Life with a Laryngectomee

A Remembrance

by Charles McKelvy

The Dunery Press

Life with a Laryngectomee: A Remembrance

Published in 2015 by The Dunery Press
Copyright 2015 by Charles McKelvy

Photograph of Hannah McKelvy by Charles McKelvy

ISBN: 978-0-944771-41-9

The Dunery Press publishes the work of Charles and
Natalie McKelvy exclusively.

To be put on our mailing list, please write us at:
The Dunery Press
P.O. Box 116
Harbert, MI 49115

For them that brought me to the dance:

My parents:

James and Hannah McKelvy

Thank you both, for encouraging me to read AND write!

Other Books by Charles McKelvy
published by The Dunery Press

The Celebrant and Other Works (2012)
Sister Hood and Other Stories (2009)
Tunnel Vision and Other Works (2007)
Bob the Weatherman and Other Works (2005)
Christmas Presence (2002)
Rogue Warbler and Other Works (2001)
The Cottage Cycle and Other Works (2000)
Baby Pictures and Other Works (1999)
Tales from the Other Side (1996)
Plays with Fire (1994)
Billy and Other Stories (1992)
Odin the Homeless and Other Stories (1990)
Chicagoland (1988)

For children:
Clash of the Cloud People (with Eric Heward) (2004)
The Iceman's Path: A Ghostly Novel (1999)
Jeremiah's Journey (with Bob Price) (1998)
Kids in the Woods (with Mike Sova) (1993)

The James Clarke novels:
Holy Orders (1989)
James II (1991)
Clarke Street (1993)
Clarke Theatre and Other Works (1995)
Clarke Theatre, (Act II) and Other Works (1997)
Clarke Barred and Other Stories (1998)

Foreword

War and drunkenness are perennial themes in Western literature, especially literature written by men about men. From the Old Testament, to the Greek classics (*The Odyssey, The Labors of Hercules*), all the way to the modern works of Dostoyevsky, Tolstoy, Faulkner, Hemingway, and many others, men always seem to be going off to fight some epic battle and then making fools of themselves with alcohol. In this memoir, a 21st-century man tries to make sense of the war and the drunkenness in his own family. It is a very human story of a child's love for his father, his desire to please him, and his failed attempts to follow in his father's footsteps, to be a real man, to be a hero.

But as you will see, the author's failure to be just like his dad is a good thing in the end. He is not able to go off and become a war hero. He is not able to drink himself to death like his father and many of his father's friends. Instead, he has to fight a different battle, create a new story, and live to tell it so that others might benefit from his experience.

This memoir will speak to you if you grew up with an alcoholic parent (or two), like Charley and myself. He read this story to me during the drive to and from a weekend retreat where we had the privilege to hang out with other men in recovery from war and alcoholism. I was struck by Charley's ability to accept his parents as they were and to find a way to forgive them and love them. That is the battle that too many of us have been unwilling to engage. As far as I can see, it is the only way our battered and broken civilization will be able to make it for another millennium. More of us must make the effort that Charley has made to straighten up and fly right, to practice love and tolerance (not just talk about it), and to cease to fight with reality. Alcoholism is and always has been a fatal illness—but there is a solution that's been working since Charley's dad went off to fight the Second World War. War is an expensive and ultimately ineffective way to settle international disputes. We have not seemed able to find an alternative yet. But clearly, it must start with each person deciding, based on their own experience, that they will choose to practice love, tolerance, and forgiveness rather than just repeat the same old tired story that men have been telling since the beginnings of recorded history. I like Charley's story better. I hope you do, too.

—*Michael Thomas Klinger, garden-variety drunk, chronic malcontent, beneficiary of unmerited grace.*

Life with a Laryngectomee

"We shall not flag or fail. We shall fight in France, we shall fight on the seas and oceans, we shall fight with growing confidence and growing strength in the air, we shall defend our island, whatever the cost may be, we shall fight on the beaches, we shall fight on the landing grounds, we shall fight in the fields and in the streets, we shall fight in the hills; we shall never surrender."

—Winston Leonard Spencer Churchill

4 June 1940

Chapter One: No Story Tonight

"Go ask your father to read to you."

I did as my mother—Hannah Dick Macfarlan McKelvy—ordered.

We're talking about late fall in 1956 here, in the *village in the city* Beverly neighborhood on the far southwest side of Chicago, and I was all of 6, and my father—James Scovel McKelvy—was all of 38.

Clutching my well-thumbed copy of *Now We Are Six* to my chest, I climbed the stairs of our Georgian-style, two-story, brick house and walked into the master bedroom ready to have Dad read to me from my favorite book.

It was way before my 3-year-old brother, Donald Adams McKelvy, and I were due in bed, so I expected to find Dad up and about, maybe at the little writing table by the window writing sales orders for the company he worked for as an industrial salesman, General Refractories Co.

But I did find it strange that Dad would do his business in the bedroom when he had a perfectly good desk downstairs, and an even more perfectly well-stocked bar in the corner of the kitchen.

Dad usually came home from selling refractory bricks to the steel mills that lined the southern rim of Lake Michigan and went right to his industrial-strength bar and had himself a scotch-on-the-rocks-with-a-twist or two or three or four or five.

But that night—and I remember it as a fall night when the darkness was beating the daylights out of the day—that night I remember something terribly amiss in the tidy little world of the Clan McKelvy at 1645 W. 106th Street, Chicago, 43, Illinois.

Despite my misgivings, I was determined to have Dad read me a story because Mom was busy with brother Donald downstairs. So I burst into the master bedroom all set for a story.

"Dad," I said, staring at all 6-plus-feet of my movie-star-handsome father splayed out on the bed, "would you read me a story?"

Dad forced a smile and said he'd give it a go.

He bid me sit on the edge of the bed, sat up and took my book, and opened it to the story I wanted to hear.

I can hear him still in my mind's ear reading the opening line.

I had been hearing that golden voice since I was being knit in my mother's womb. Dad's voice was the rich, reassuring call that coaxed his first-born into the "A-Atlantic" Ocean at Ship Bottom, New Jersey and Lake Michigan at Rainbow Beach in Chicago.

Dad spoke that night in the same resonant tenor tone that had risen in laughter on Friday nights in our apartment in South Shore when he had his buddies over to watch *The Friday Night Fights* on that new-fangled thing called television and to drink beers out of the bottle and smoke endless unfiltered cigarettes.

I can hear that voice still, and, still, I cannot for the life of me hear it as it really was.

Sadly, Dad refused to record his golden voice, and my mind's ear will only let me hear it as through a cocktail glass darkly.

Dad's voice sounded like amber looks to me now.

It was rich and deep and dark and as lovely as any man's voice can ever be.

Our ancestors from Ireland and Scotland and England called to me that night in Dad's voice.

I heard them all and I heard my dear, dear Daddy reading to me from my favorite book, and then—

And then Dad dropped my book and grabbed a bloody handkerchief I hadn't noticed and coughed more crimson blood into it.

Dad coughed and coughed and, oh, how he coughed.

There would be no story that night.

But there would be this story to tell.

Chapter Two: The First Landing

I have to tell you about both sets of stairs we had in our house at 1645 W. 106th Street before we proceed with the rest of the remembrance. (Excuse me, we actually had three sets of stairs in our house, if you count the folding set that dropped down from the attic, but those don't really figure into our narrative.)

For our purposes, the two relevant sets were:

1. The stairs from the second floor—where we had our three bedrooms (more on those later) and the master bath—to the main floor with our living room, dining room, breakfast nook, powder room, kitchen, and (more-or-less) heated sun porch.

2. The precipitous steps up from the basement with its poured concrete floor, load-bearing pillars, washer and dryer, and two storage rooms, one of which was converted from the coal bin that had been used by previous owners.

But first to the main stairs which figure prominently into our present discussion.

Simple really:

-First flight of three or four stairs;

-The first landing where you turned sharply to the right and prepared to descend the—

-Long flight of stairs to—

-The second landing, which faced the living room and led to—

-The third flight of three or four stairs, or stoop, if you will.

The first landing was for eavesdropping on the grown-ups in the living room, and the second landing was for command performances for the grown-ups in the living room. And trust me when I say there were always grown-ups in the living room doing what grown-ups always did at 1645 W. 106th Street, which was to drink Dad's booze down to the last golden drop. Dad didn't call the place *Mac's Bar & Grill* for nothin'.

Having set the stage, we will now lift the curtain on Dad's last night with his natural voice.

The living room was full of grown-ups doing what they always did in our living room: drink Dad's booze down to the last golden drop.

Having been taught that "children are to be seen and not heard," my brother Donald Adams and I greeted the "guesties" and then retreated to the first landing there better to hear the drama unfold.

Now, I know that Mother had taken us aside and explained exactly what was wrong with Dad: his sore throat was more than a sore throat. Seriously more.

More like carcinoma of the larynx.

Bad.

Very bad.

But Mom's good-old Uncle Douglas Macfarlan back in Philadelphia had been consulted because he was a leading ear/nose/throat physician, and he had recommended the best of his best colleagues in Chicago to perform a total laryngectomy on Dad. Meaning that Doctor Lauren Holinger was going to remove Dad's voice-producing vocal cords and attach his trachea, or windpipe, to a surgically created opening in his neck known as a stoma.

Dad, Mom explained, would have to find a whole new way of talking, hopefully by using his esophagus to carry voice-producing sounds into his mouth. This was all new and quite frightening to Mom, of course, but I know she told us that speech experts were telling them that the ability to learn esophageal speech varies from individual to individual and may take anywhere from a month to two years or longer.

The key to mastering esophageal speech is sustained burping, Mom said, and Mom just wondered if Dad was going to be up for it.

I think all this was over my 3-year-old brother's head, and I know it just upset me no end and caused me to worry that my dear Daddy was about to become some kind of scary freak monster with a frog/dragon voice.

This was 1956, mind you, and children were expected to be seen and not heard, so there didn't seem to be a whole lot of doting over Yours Truly and his delicate psyche.

Suck it up, Charley me boy!

Right?

Right!

All I remember about going into the night before Dad's operation is that I was totally freaked and I was trying not to freak out my poor little brother who knew in his 3-year-old soul that our ship was taking on water.

But then the grown-ups came to fill up our living room on the eve of destruction, and there was comfort in that company of friends who had been gained from our days in the South Shore neighborhood when war-weary begetters of the Baby Boom began to get together socially. Steel was the lingua franca that formed those friendships of a lifetime that followed us from South Shore when we moved to Beverly in time for my sixth birthday on May 7, 1956. The mills were as close as South Works over on 79th Street and the lake, and many of the men worked for the steel companies, or, like Dad, sold products to them.

Dad always liked to quote that line from Shakespeare's *Hamlet* in which Polonius counsels his sons to bind their friends to themselves "with hoops of steel." Dad proudly displayed a Beta Theta Pi mug with that quote inscribed on it over his bar.

So Dad and Mom were binding their steely friends to themselves that night in January 1957 with hoops of steel and copious amounts of scotch and soda, vodka and vermouth, gin and tonic.

I remember sitting there on the first landing with my brother, listening to them down there in the living room encouraging Dad and telling him all would be well and sharing stories of others who had overcome adversities.

But, you know, I do not remember but a single word of what my father said.

I do remember that his friends begged him to tape-record his golden voice for posterity. To make an audible record for his family.

This was 1957, after all, and if we were capable of incinerating the planet with hydrogen bombs, we could certainly make a high-fidelity recording of Dad's natural voice with a neighbor's fancy reel-to-reel tape recorder. All right, they weren't portable and the playthings of every proletariat, but they were available, and they were being offered to our family that very night.

I remember the begging and cajoling.

"Please, Jimmy."

"For your family, Jimmy."

"You have a beautiful voice, Jimmy."

And so on and so forth until Dad said the one and only word that I truly remember him saying in his natural voice: "No."

Just "no" and nevermore would I hear my Daddy speak in his natural voice again.

Chapter Three: Post Op

Picture, if you will, a dismally gray Sunday afternoon in January 1957 in Chicago.

Brother Donald and I are being driven north from Beverly in a Chevrolet piloted by "Uncle Tom" and "Aunt Lou" Bartlett. They are not blood relatives, but we honor them with familiar titles because Uncle Tom is Dad's boss at General Refractories and Aunt Lou is always there when Mom needs to board her boys. In fact, we had been boarded at the Bartlett house over there on Wood Street just south of 107th Street and made to play nicely with the three Bartlett children: Tom "Tee," Reynolds "Renny," and Shelley.

Aunt Lou has been especially sweet and solicitous, because she knows we are in for one **TRIPLE WHAMMO** of a change to our routine. I recall extra servings of pancakes and sausage at the Bartlett house that morning, and I don't think Tee tormented us at all that day.

We were, in a word, special.

Handle with care.

These boys are in for it, so do not aggravate them or poke their eyes out.

No one poked our eyes out, and so we were wide-eyed and taking it all in as we were being driven north and east on such streets as Vincennes, and 79th, and Indiana. Uncle Tom and Aunt Lou told us we would not be allowed to go up and see Dad once we got to Saint Luke's Hospital just south of the Loop on Michigan Avenue. But, they said, we would be able to stand on the sidewalk and look up at him as he waved down at us from his room.

That was to be it.

And that was it.

All of it.

"Well, here we are," Aunt Lou said.

And so we climbed out of that big Chevrolet and walked through the slush to a point just below Dad's window on some upper floor of that imposing slab of modern medicine, and, when Dad appeared in a white robe with miles and miles of white dressings around his throat, told: "Wave at your Daddy, boys."

Wave at our Daddy we did, and wave back at us our Daddy did.

And then we went back to the Bartlett's to await the next act.

Chapter Four: Billy

This is where the story goes to the dogs, or one particular dog named Billy. We did have another dog, Cindy, but she did not appear on the scene until 1968. Cindy was a stray, who appeared at a girlfriend's cottage in Indiana after a severe thunderstorm, and I brought her home, and, incredibly, Dad allowed Cindy to stay. In fact, he grew to be quite fond of her, so, it can be said that old guys do learn new dogs.

Amazing.

Anyway, our present discussion concerns Billy, so let us consider the "liver-eyed" runt from the neighbor's litter of springer spaniels who came to live with us at 1645 W. 106th Street before Dad's operation.

He was my dog, and so I got to name him, and I named him for my best friend back in South Shore, Billy Melish.

The son of a minister, Billy Melish lived across the street from our apartment building in a real house, and I used to go over there and watch the *Mickey Mouse Club* with my best friend, and when Billy dared me to do it, I went up to the tiny screen of their television and kissed Annette Funicello on the lips. Then I dared Billy to kiss Annette, and he did it, too, and when his Mom caught us, she yelled a little but laughed more.

I liked Billy, and he liked me, and then one day he said his Dad was being posted to another church over by the Mississippi River, and they would be leaving soon, but he said I should just head on over and we could go rafting together down the Mighty Miss just like Huck Finn and Jim.

But that never happened, and I never saw Billy Melish again, but I sure did miss him, and so when I was given a dog from the neighbor's litter of springer pups, why I named him Billy. And I told my four-legged friend Billy that I would never let him move away on me. We would be together 'til the day one of us died.

Hah!!!

When I look at family photos of me and Billy I always see that I am clinging desperately to Billy. And I was, because I remember being told by my mother to keep Billy away from

Dad and not to let him jump on little Donald Adams and to clean up his messes pronto or he would "be given to the next passing Indian."

That's right, even before Dad's surgery, Billy's tenure was in doubt.

I remember being banished to the basement with Billy after Billy got too frisky upstairs. Yes, dare I say, I remember Dad, my dear Daddy, kicking Billy down those precipitous basement steps.

I remember Billy whimpering at the bottom of the steps, and I remember racing down to him and hugging him to me and telling him that we were going to run away to the Mississippi River and raft all the way down to New Orleans with my best friend in the whole world, Billy Melish.

Yeah, right.

The chances of going to see the Melishs over by the Mississippi River were as good as Dad shutting down *Mac's Bar & Grill* up there in the living room.

Some people who only knew my father later in his life rationalized his—dare I say—heavy drinking because he was a laryngectomee.

You would drink and drink and drink and drink if you were a laryngectomee like Jimmy McKelvy and somebody carved a hole in your neck and—

I get ahead of myself, when what I need is to clearly state for the record: Dad did not start drinking the day after his surgery.

Oh no!

I was there.

I know what went on night after night after night after night before Dad's date with Dr. Lauren Holinger in January 1957.

It takes one to know one, and this one writing this narrative is a stone-cold alcoholic. A recovering, stone-cold alcoholic, but a stumble-bum drunk if ever there was one, and I saw my father routinely drink to excess long before they scalloped out his throat at that Gothic-revival hall of medicine on South Michigan Avenue known as Saint Luke's Hospital.

That's my story, and I'm stickin' with it.

Okay, so Billy's days with us were numbered from the git-go, plain and simple, and I do remember Dad kicking the dog the mean girl from next door called "Liver Eyes" down the basement steps, and I do remember cowering in the basement with Billy while the grown-ups were growling with drunken delight upstairs in *Mac's Bar & Grill*, long before that surgeon took a knife to my Daddy's throat.

Dad, as far as I know, didn't have a dog when he was growing up in a "Mainline" suburb of Philadelphia, and I do not recall him saying any more about me having a dog than: "Keep that damn dog out from underfoot, or he's gone."

So Billy was mine, living on borrowed time.

And then came Dad's surgery—the aforementioned total laryngectomy to remove his voice-producing vocal cords and attach his trachea, or windpipe, to that perforation in his neck called a stoma.

Oh yeah, baby!

Oh yeah!

So, friends in Florida invited us down to the Sunshine State to recover from Dad's ordeal, and Mom and Dad accepted.

The plan was for the four of us to fly down to Florida from Chicago Midway Airport on Eastern Airlines, and then we would stay in a cottage and Dad would recuperate with Mom while my brother and I went for boat rides with these family friends who had moved down to Florida from Philadelphia.

Florida.

In winter.

Great.

What's not to like?

Except Mom said we had to board Billy with the vet over on Western Avenue near 99th Street.

She promised me that we would get Billy just as soon as we got back from Florida.

Only we didn't.

When we got back from Florida, I asked: "Mom, are we going to get Billy today?"

"Not today, Charley. I'm busy. Maybe tomorrow."

Just play that tape another week until finally Mom got fed up with my persistence and said: "Look, the vet is giving Billy to a good home because he's too much for your father. After all he's been through. End of story."

Gotcha, Mom.

Chapter Five: The Lady in White

Our new life without Dad's natural voice.

Was I upset by any of this?

Was I coping?

Well, when we changed planes in Atlanta on our way back from Florida on good-old Eastern Airlines, we went into the terminal, and everybody but me used the "facilities."

I was told to wait outside the ladies' room for Mom to come out with Donald Adams, while Dad went to the gents by his lonesome. I know what I was told to do, but I was so flustered that I took off walking in that walking forest of quick-marching adults, in search of my Daddy.

I quickly became lost and confused and frightened and upset and—there was a tall, handsome man wearing the smart uniform of an Eastern Airlines pilot bending down to ask me if I was lost.

"Yes, I am!!!"

And, do you know, that wonderful pilot/man took me by the hand and led me to my poor, frantic mother who had come out of the lavatory with Donald Adams expecting to find me waiting where she had told me to wait.

But, no, there was no sign of little Charles Kenneth.

He gone!

Seriously gone swimming off into that turbulent sea of passengers.

So, yes, Mom was upset when the pilot brought me to her, and Dad was upset, too, when he joined the scene, but, obviously, he could not express his displeasure because he was missing his natural voice.

Yes, our new life without Dad's natural voice.

And finding a voice for Dad is precisely where we will begin, and we will look in our living room at "grown-up" time in early 1957 when the only grown-up visiting us that night was the woman in white. And by us, I do mean the whole, entire family, including Dad, Mom, Yours Truly, Donald Adams, and Mary Louise, who had been forming in Mom's womb since our restorative trip to Florida.

I don't think Mary Louise heard a word of what the woman in white told us that night, but I have always believed that she felt the raw energy of our family in crisis.

And the living room was positively charged that night when the woman in white appeared because she was a beautician—hence the white outfit—who had come straight from work to share her experience, strength, and hope as a recovering laryngectomee. More specifically, as one who had mastered esophageal speech, which, as you may recall from our earlier discussion, requires sustained burping.

Dad was showing no enthusiasm for sustained burping, and, indeed, he was telling us with his terse memos that he was not expecting much from the visit by this woman in white, whom I recall was named Frances.

Frances what, I don't remember, but I can see her coming in through the front door and greeting us in what I still think of as her *burp voice.*

Imagine a 6-year-old hearing a lovely lady in white speaking in a burp voice.

And, please, imagine you were there with us that night.

Dad has had his throat cut up one side and down the other and is breathing through a hole in his neck, and Mom has one in the oven as a result of our family get-away to Florida, the oldest is fresh from the humiliating experience of being presented to his fellow second-graders at Alice L. Barnard Elementary School at 104th and Charles (that's right, Charles!!!) by his kindly teacher, who then tells the class that his father has just undergone an operation to remove a cancerous growth from his throat and will no longer have a natural voice, and number-two child—3-year-old Donald Adams— is mutely watching all this unfold with wide eyes and a stuffed monkey—Mr. Monkey—clutched tightly to his chest.

For once there are no other grown-ups—or "guesties"— than this Frances woman in white.

So all eyes and ears are on her as she proceeds at the behest of Dad's surgeon to encourage him to start working on his sustained burping so he can communicate with esophageal speech instead of terse memos.

Well, Dad's eyes were not on this Frances lady for long.

I remember the far-away look on his face.

And then the anger.

Dad was not buying it.

No, sir!

Dad was barely controlling his notorious anger, and had he still had his natural voice, he would have exploded in a cannonade of caustic expletives.

Oh yeah!

Not a fun night for the McKelvy family.

But our lady in white was not to be deterred by her fellow laryngectomee's reticence.

Quite the contrary.

Frances just kept burping up intelligible words of encouragement, and Mom and brother Donald and I just kept nodding encouragingly at Dad and hoping and praying that he would give esophageal speech a run for the money.

But Dad didn't.

No way, José.

Dad heard Frances out, and when she was finally gone, he made it clear in gestures and writing that he was not going to be a burping fool.

He had another way, a way suggested by a man who had come to see him in the hospital after his surgery, and he wrote the one word that would resound in our ears for the rest of Dad's natural life:

ELECTROLARYNX, aka: The Voice Box.

Chapter Six: The Voice Box

Google *electrolarynx* and *Wikipedia, the free encyclopedia* will promptly tell you "an *electrolarynx*, sometimes referred to as a 'throat back', is a medical device about the size of a small electric razor used to produce clearer speech by those who have lost their voicebox, usually due to cancer of the larynx. The most common device is a handheld, battery-operated device placed under the mandible which produces vibrations and allows speech."

There you have it, sports fans: Dad's electrolarynx from Chicago-based Aurex Corporation.

When Aurex's Ted Huth visited Dad in the hospital and demonstrated his wonderful device, Dad was delighted.

With the electrolarynx there was a way forward with a voice we could all understand.

I remember hearing Dad talk for the first time with his electrolarynx. Yes, it looked like he was about to shave his neck with an electric razor and then he pushed the button and this buzzing sound went up his throat and when he moved his lips, perfectly formed words issued forth.

EUREKA!!!!

That was not what Dad said on that maiden voyage.

No, I seem to remember in my mind's ear hearing him say something like: "Can you hear me?"

Could we hear him?

Could we understand him?

Every golden word.

Yes, Dad was sounding mechanical and unnatural, but he was speaking complete sentences and smiling, and I know Mom was crying, and then I was crying, and little Donald Adams was smiling and crying, and our unborn sister (Mary Louise) was probably doing back-flips in Mom's womb.

That was the moment!!!

Dad had a new voice.

A new voice box.

THE VOICE BOX!!!!!!

There was no turning back.

Engines full ahead!

Dad, after all, had served as a naval officer in Utility Squadron Fifteen at U.S. Naval Air Station, Brunswick, Maine during World War II, after first serving briefly in both the U.S. Marine Corps and the U.S. Army, so he was all about steaming fearlessly into enemy waters.

He had flown over the Atlantic Ocean searching for German submarines during the war, and he could quote the passage from Churchill's famous wartime speech that serves as the epigram for this book. Dad would never surrender to his voicelessness.

NEVER!!!!!

He would fight it with growing confidence and growing strength on the beaches, on the landing grounds, in the fields, and in the streets, and in the hills, and in *Mac's Bar & Grill*, and he would never surrender.

And he never did, thanks to that handheld device Ted Huth showed him how to use after he underwent radical neck surgery in 1957.

Dad had so, so much to say, and, then, he had a new voice—what we would soon come to call *the voice box*—with which to say it.

But it was not always the voice others wanted to hear, which brings us to the next chapter in the story: Greasers.

Chapter Seven: Greasers

If there is one episode that best describes the horrible reaction some insensitive boors had to Dad's new, artificial voice, it was what happened over east at the driving range on Halsted Street at, oh say, 115th Street where Dad was determined to teach his two boys the game of their Scottish ancestors—golf.

The driving range was owned and operated by a famous golfer of the day, but, for the life of me, I cannot remember his name.

Oh well.

But I can picture Dad up there in heaven just shaking his angelic head at me.

I am sure my brother Donald could remember the name, because he took to golf from the git-go. He listened to Dad's advice, kept his head down, followed all the way through, and thwacked ball after ball straight down range, almost to the railroad tracks on the other side of the fence.

Brother Donald was—and is—a natural. He clearly inherited the Scottish golf gene.

I, on the other hand, clearly did not.

And so I frustrated Dear Old Dad no end that day at the driving range named for the famous golfer whose name I cannot remember by lifting my head mid-swing and utterly failing to follow through, stroke after stroke after stroke.

I learned the meaning of *hook* and *slice* that day, but, for the life of me, I cannot remember which of those two cardinal golf sins I committed the most.

Hooking?

Maybe.

Slicing?

Probably.

I don't know, but I do know that Dad was quickly losing his patience with his oldest son, and so he let me know in certain terms that I was "never going to learn the game of golf if—"

And that's when they started laughing.

And pointing.

And laughing until they were red in the face.

And pointing until their fingers were quivering.

GREASERS!

Oh yeah!

The real deal.

And they were having one righteous yuck at the Old Man's new voice. They called it a *robot voice,* and they just kept on laughing and pointing as we went about our driving lesson.

I wanted to kill them, and I am sure brother Donald did, too.

How dare they laugh and point at our Daddy just because he had to talk by holding an electrolarynx against his neck?

They were smoking cigarettes: didn't they know that the same thing could happen to them?

Didn't they know what Dad had been through?

Didn't they know what he had lost?

Didn't they know how relieved and happy our family was to have Dad back on speaking terms?

No, they were high-school greasers in blue jeans and tight t-shirts with enough petroleum products in their hair to keep Saudia Arabia solvent for centuries. And, as earlier indicated, they were smoking.

And they thought we had brought our disabled Dad with his *robot voice* to the driving range—clearly their driving range—expressly for their amusement.

My brother and I might have wanted to kill them, but our father—the object of their ignorant scorn—our father just let their cruel laughter roll over him like water off a duck's back.

Water off a duck's back.

That's just the way that cruel laughter rolled off Dad.

Like he didn't even hear it.

As if, well, as if he was thinking of one of his favorite poems: *If—* by Rudyard Kipling.

Dad told us without saying a word that day that the world was full of fools like those guffawing greasers, and that it became us—in the words of Rudyard Kipling—to keep our heads about us while others about us were losing theirs and blaming it on us.

Dad, in his silence and confidence, taught us strength that day.

And he taught us to read and to heed the advice of Rudyard Kipling, which, if you will permit me, I will recite for you now in my father's memory:

If—
by Rudyard Kipling

If you can keep your head when all about you
Are losing theirs and blaming it on you,
If you can trust yourself when all men doubt you,
But make allowance for their doubting too;
If you can wait and not be tired by waiting,
Or being lied about, don't deal in lies,
Or being hated, don't give way to hating,
And yet don't look too good, nor talk too wise:

If you can dream—and not make dreams your master;
If you can think—and not make thoughts your aim;
If you can meet with Triumph and Disaster
And treat those two impostors the same;
If you can bear to hear the truth you've spoken
Twisted by knaves to make a trap for fools,
Or watch the things you gave your life to, broken,
And stoop and build 'em up with worn-out tools:

If you can make one heap of all your winnings
And risk it on one turn of pitch-and-toss,
And lose, and start again at your beginnings
And never breathe a word about your loss,
If you can force your heart and nerve and sinew
To serve your turn long after they are gone,
And so hold on when there is nothing in you
Except the Will which says to them: 'Hold on!'

If you can talk with crowds and keep your virtue,
Or walk with Kings—nor lose the common touch,
If neither foes nor loving friends can hurt you,
If all men count with you, but none too much;
If you can fill the unforgiving minute
With sixty seconds' worth of distance run,
Yours is the Earth and everything that's in it,
And—which is more—you'll be a Man, my son!

Chapter Eight: We Were Not Alone

For Christians, hope is a virtue, but for the ancient Greeks, it was a vice.

Sadly, it was the ancient Greeks who had the last word that Sunday afternoon in 1957 when we drove to a near western suburb—I'm remembering Berwyn, for some reason—for a meeting of laryngectomees and their families.

It was Dr. Holinger, I am sure, who had urged Dad to attend.

Get involved.

Take the family.

You don't have to suffer by yourself.

You are not in this alone.

You are not the only one who lost his voice to cancer.

Find your tribe and join the fellowship.

Share your experience, hope, and strength with others of your ilk.

You know the drill.

We all know the routine now that 12-step programs and recovery one-day-at-a-time and letting go and letting God and all that good, orderly direction has been plastered on the walls of contemporary culture.

But 1957?

Not so much.

At least not so much in our car as we drove relentlessly north and west to some restaurant in Berwyn, or some similar suburb, in search of a little serenity and fellowship.

Well, let me tell you:

There was tension a plenty in our car that afternoon as Dad drove us to this meeting his doctor wanted him to attend.

He did not want to go.

Plain and simple.

Mom, on the other hand, really, really wanted Dad to go.

I wanted him to go. Donald Adams wanted Dad to commune with other laryngectomees.

We three were of one mind, and I am sure our sister Mary Louise was waving her arms in Mom's womb and shouting:

"You go, Dad!"

But Dad did not want to go, and he was letting us all know through his angry driving and red-faced fulminations, with and without his electrolarynx.

And it didn't help any that I—who was seated in the passenger seat so Mom could be with brother Donald in the backseat—started laughing hysterically.

Yes, I was hysterical.

I have completed a fearless and searching moral inventory of myself, and I can assure you that there is a file marked: *Hysteria. (See 1957 drive to Berwyn)*

Oh yeah.

Without putting too fine a point on it, allow me to say that I allowed my upset over the whole experience of watching my father lose his voice to cancer to, well, to upset me to the point of hysterical laughter.

And so I laughed hysterically as my increasingly angry father drove us to a date with a destiny he was determined to deny.

Long before we got there.

But get there we did, and what awaited us in that banquet hall in Berwyn was a whole lot of eastern European food and daddies just like our Daddy with holes in their necks and electrolarynxes and sustained burping and supportive family members ready to support the newcomer and his hopeful family members.

But, you know, I don't remember Dad digging it at all.

I do remember Mom being oh so hopeful and urgently supportive.

As in: "Come on, Jimmy, listen to these people. Hear what they have to say."

Uh uh.

Dad was not digging it at all.

But brother Donald and I were.

We realized the second we walked into that banquet room that smelled deliciously of sauerkraut and spicy sausage that there were kids just like us who knew exactly what it was to be just like us.

Kids like us who had been laughed at and stared at and ridiculed by greasers and—

It was just such an amazing relief that I never, ever wanted to leave that warm and savory banquet hall in Berwyn, or a suburb just like Berwyn.

I wanted to become an instant eastern European and eat sauerkraut and spicy sausage and dumplings and cabbage and fart and laugh with the other kids whose new normal was a dad with a hole in his neck.

That's what I wanted.

And I remember talking to a kid there about pets.

He asked me if we had a pet, and I said: "Oh no, laryngectomees can't have pets. It's too much for them."

And he laughed and replied: "Oh no, after my father's operation, he went out and got a puppy for me. He said we needed a puppy in the house."

I was—and still am—stunned.

Needless to say, we didn't run out and get a puppy to replace Billy when we got home that day.

When we got home that day, some us of realized that the ancient Greeks were absolutely right: hope is a vice not a virtue.

For we never, ever, went back to that banquet hall to hang out with other laryngectomees.

Dad wanted no part of that, thank you very much.

Not when he had all the fellowship he needed at *Mac's Bar & Grill.*

Thank you very much.

Chapter Nine: *Mac's Bar & Grill*

Dad was determined to recover at home, particularly at home in our living room, which as you know only too well by now, was known in the neighborhood as *Mac's Bar & Grill*.

So why don't we look in now at *Mac's Bar & Grill* back in 1957 to see how we were all dealing with that megaton bomb dropped on us called cancer of the larynx?

But wait, you say, how can you call it *Mac's Bar & Grill* if it was just your living room?

Good question.

How's this for an answer:

There was this wholesale liquor store in the Loop in those days called Zimmerman's that delivered to the bars on Western Avenue. Booze by the truckload.

Never a surprise to see a Zimmerman's truck unloading the goodies at one of those establishments on the west side of Western Avenue.

Nor was it a surprise to see a Zimmerman's truck pull into our driveway once a week and dispense a week's worth of scotch, gin, vodka, vermouth, club soda, tonic, and ginger ale. The latter wasn't just for us kids; it was for the ladies who liked sweet drinks.

Okay, so are you satisfied that we called it *Mac's Bar & Grill* because it was stocked by a wholesale liquor store in the Loop?

I hope so, and if you're not, please read on, and you'll soon agree that our living room was worthy of the moniker that Dad gave it, and fondly called it as he was standing in front of the picture window in the center of the living room with a drink—scotch-on-the-rocks in winter and gin-and-tonic in summer—in one hand and his voice box in the other.

That was the signal, you see to—

But, wait, I get ahead of myself.

Armed with his electrolarynx, Dad was able to go back to work for General Refractories at 208 S. LaSalle Street in the Loop, but his boss, Tom Bartlett, mainly had him do his sales work from the office rather than send him out to the mills where he could not be heard over the din of steel-making. Although we do have to credit Ted Huth of Aurex for equipping Dad with a high-volume electrolarynx for sales work. Unfortunately, that did not work out for Dad.

Anyway, Dad worked downtown and commuted on the old Rock Island Line from 107th and Hale, and in the evening—'round about supper time—he would round the corner at 106th and Wood and march east on 106th Street.

We'd be out playing with our pals in front of the house, and when we spotted him lumbering our way, we would frantically police the yard and then tear into the house and set up the bar in Dad's corner of the kitchen complete with filling the ice bucket and setting out the tools and bottles and making sure—absolutely sure—that there was enough of everything for *the guesties.*

That's right: *the guesties.*

Hey, Stephen King, there's a title for your next tome: *The Guesties.*

Anyway, we were on it the inkling we saw Dad turn onto 106th Street way out there at Wood. We ate lots of carrots in those days, so we had keen eyes.

Yeah, right.

Hey, we were sharp-eyed of necessity because you didn't want the Old Man to catch you with his bar down.

No, sir!

So Dad would walk from Wood Street to Drew Street and then a third of a block to our house at 1645 W. 106th Street, and he would always stop and inspect the yard for stray sticks and acorns fallen from the oak tree on our front lawn. Woe to us if he found a twig we had missed, or, if he found a branch that one of those pesky squirrels had deliberately dislodged in the time between our policing and Dad's arrival.

If we failed lawn patrol, Dad would scowl, and enter scowling, and he would berate us the second he saw us standing at attention just inside the front door, like cowering recruits in boot camp.

Well, having later been a cowering recruit in boot camp, I can safely say that the comparison is apt.

Quite apt.

So Dad would unload on his two deadbeat boys and then he would march into the bar—well, kitchen and bar—and inspect our handiwork there. If all were quiet, we would take a breath or two.

If not, we would hop to in the kitchen and get whatever we had forgotten to put out.

Pronto.

And I do mean pronto.

Then Dad would make himself a stiff one with a heavy hand on either the scotch or gin.

Glug, glug, glug.

Dad would take a satisfying sip, pronounce himself right with the world, and then proceed to the picture window where he would raise his glass with one hand and his electrolarynx with the other. The former was to signal our across-the-street neighbor, the irrepressible Elizabeth "Pudah" Peebles, that *Mac's Bar & Grill* was open for the night, and the latter was to tell me: "Go and help your Aunt Pudah across the street."

She wasn't really our aunt, but we called her Aunt Pudah, because she loomed so large in our lives on a daily basis. You're probably wondering where *Pudah* came from and where Pudah's husband, Jim Peebles, was.

Well, I can only say that Pudah always said she had been called that since she was a little girl, and she always said that her husband—whom we called Uncle Jim—was still at work.

As in—well—I don't want to tell tales out of school.

Suffice it to say Pudah was always waiting in her living room for the signal from Jimmy McKelvy that *Mac's Bar & Grill* was open for the night.

And there I would be at her front door gallantly offering my 6-year-old arm.

What a little gent I was.

I swear.

Aunt Pudah would inevitably be dressed for the evening in a loose dress of Hawaiian origin, the famous *muumuu*. Aunt Pudah's muumuus were always something sensational to behold because they beheld one buxom lady with a libido that didn't quit. And, as a quick aside, let me tell you of the time Aunt Pudah had fallen and bruised her thigh and wanted to show us the full extent of her injury. So she hiked up her muumuu and not only showed us the full extent of her injury but a full frontal view of a part of the female anatomy I had only seen in my dreams.

Okay, so there would be Aunt Pudah in one of her spangly, sparkly muumuus and enough red lipstick and eye make-up to keep MGM in business for years. Oh, and her spikey-heeled house slippers. Why, I think she even had a pair in faux leopard skin. Or was that her muumuu, or both?

Probably both.

Okay, so there would Pudah Peebles be on her front porch ready for little Charley McKelvy to escort her across the street. And, folks, we're talking neighborhood cow path here, not some bustling through-street like 107th or Western.

Aunt Pudah would invariably lean down so I could get an unobstructed view of her package and plant a wet smacker on my cheek. Then she would invite me to reciprocate by saying: "Give your Aunt Pudah a kiss, sweetie."

And I would.

Would I ever.

Wouldn't you?

Then I would escort Aunt Pudah across 106th Street, after looking both ways, of course, and that would be the signal for the third leg of this little love triangle to haul himself on over to *Mac's Bar & Grill* from his house next door to *Mac's Bar & Grill.*

Himself being the one, the only John "Big John" Matunas.

One of Chicago's finest, Big John was assigned to a district on the West Side. He would often return home while on duty and park his cruiser in his driveway with the windows down and the radio on, just in case he got a call as he stripped down to his dago-t and trotted out his industrial-strength bottle of bourbon with the pump-action neck and drink the day away while we kids carried on as best we could as neighborhood kids. Big John loved to tease us kids about the gorilla that escaped from the zoo, but we always figured he was the gorilla who escaped from the West Side where he was supposed to be upholding the law and keeping order. Let's just say he was aptly nicknamed.

And, so you know, Big John never told us to call him *Uncle John*. He was always Mr. Matunas, and, yes, he was a larger-than-life Lithuanian-American with a spirited, Irish-American wife named Helen and a son and daughter. His daughter, in fact, was the one who dubbed my dog Billy "Liver Eyes." She thought that was hysterical, and so did the rest of the kids on the block, and Beverly being the Irish-Catholic enclave that it was in the 1950s, there were plenty of kids on the block.

So on with the show at *Mac's Bar & Grill,* and let's just say that Dad would light up like a kid on Christmas morning when his two favorite people in the whole world showed up in *Mac's Bar & Grill* for a night of flowing drinks and Benny Goodman tunes on the high-fi.

Aunt Pudah and Big John had no trouble with Dad's voice box or his operation or his stoma or his being a laryngectomee.

They accepted him exactly as he was, without reservation.

They were his support group.

Others would appear at *Mac's Bar & Grill*, often neighbors Dad had seen on the train, but none were as regular as Aunt Pudah Peebles and Big John Matunas.

They were such regulars, that Mom once said to Pudah: "If I see you and John Matunas in this living room together, I am not going to regard it as a coincidence."

And it was no coincidence that Aunt Pudah and Big John had come to help Dad drain his liquor supply on a daily basis so the Zimmerman's truck would have to return on a weekly basis.

There's so, so much more to say about *Mac's Bar & Grill* and the role it played in Dad's recovery and in our family life, and I will say it in forthcoming chapters as I remember my life with a laryngectomee.

But first, I must complete our family picture with the arrival of my sister, Mary Louise, on Sunday, October 13, 1957.

Chapter Ten: Now We Are Five

How do I remember that my sister Mary Louise, the youngest of the three McKelvy children, was born on a Sunday?

Simple really:

Brother Donald and I had been left to the capable care of Aunt Lou and Uncle Tom Bartlett over on Wood Street just south of 107th while Mom and Dad went to Passavant Hospital just north of the Loop to usher in their third and final child.

We McKelvy boys were out in the Bartlett backyard—and we're talking a serious backyard here—playing football with the Bartlett boys and other kids from their neighborhood when Aunt Lou appeared on the back porch and hollered: "You boys have a baby sister!"

We were delighted, but I couldn't help wondering if Dad would be, too.

Turns out he wasn't.

Turns out having a newborn, crying baby in the house was a buzz kill for the proprietor of *Mac's Bar & Grill.*

I wish I had pleasant memories of those weeks and months after my sister's birth, but aside from that day when we charged our friends a nickel to see our new baby sister and a dime to have one of our babysitter's cupcakes, I shudder to think of Dad's reaction to our sister's crying in the crib, which if memory serves correctly, was placed in the corner of the living room—smack dab in *Mac's Bar & Grill.*

Mary Louise, being a baby at the time, would do what babies did at the time, which was to cry.

Dad, being Dad at the time, would do what Dad did at the time, which was to grab his voice box and yell at Mom to "shut that kid up!"

Sometimes Dad didn't even have to grab his voice box.

Sometimes he automatically mastered esophageal speech right then and there.

We got the message either way.

Pronto.

And this is not easy for me to say, but I'll say it anyway: I most certainly saved my sister from grievous bodily harm on more than one occasion by snatching her out of her crib and whisking her to a safe corner of the house.

Dad liked to tell Aunt Pudah and Big John that he had successfully fathered a daughter because his surgery had been above the waist not below it, but that was about as light as I remember him getting with my sister's presence in the house, particularly in *Mac's Bar & Grill*.

So, yes, we were five.

We were alive.

And on edge.

Alert.

Ready for Mary Louise to cry and Dad to erupt.

As Dad liked to say on Christmas morning after his inevitable Christmas Eve, booze-fueled tirade: "It was the booze talkin'. 'Nuf said."

'Nuf said, indeed!

Chapter Eleven: *A Man's A Man For A' That*

Robert Burns got it right when he wrote: *A Man's a Man for a' that.*

Although my father wasn't one for quoting Scotland's national bard, he favored that line from the 1795 Burns poem.

Dad was indeed a man's man, for a' that and more.

And lest I present too bleak a memory of my father the laryngectomee, let me harken back to a summer day in—oh say—1959 when my pals and I were hanging out at our favorite corner—the intersection of 106th and Drew.

It was right down the block from our house, and it had a green mail-storage box upon which we would climb and pretend to be riding horses and piloting fighter planes over the shattered skies of 1940s Germany and Japan. There was a tree that bore some strange fruit, little orange berries that we never troubled ourselves to properly identify. But we decided it was safe to eat them if we first sprayed them with the leading antiseptic of the day. And, as far as I know, none of the old gang ever died from eating those orange berries.

There was almost no traffic on either 106th or Drew, so we had the actual intersection to ourselves for hours of such games of our own invention as: *Runner & Rider, Ambush with Acorns, Ambush with Snowballs, Ambush with Orange Berries,* and *Four-Corner Relay.*

None of the neighbors seemed to mind our loud presence at 106th and Drew, except for *the fireman.*

He and his wife lived in a brick house on the northwest corner of 106th and Drew. If they had children of their own, we never saw them, and if he was still working, we never saw him go to work.

He was old and crabby and, I believe, of German descent.

We kids—we spawn of the Greatest Generation—we had no use for Krauts in 1959.

They were the bums our dads had bombed to rubble and beaten back from the beachheads.

They were the enemy, and this Kraut guy on the corner—this guy we simply called *Kraut*—had clearly been planted there so we could torment him no end.

And on that particular day one of our ringleaders decided the day's game was: *Sniper Attack on Kraut.*

To illustrate how the game was to be played, he picked up some pebbles from the curb and ran over to Kraut's side of the street and flung them at the metal panel on Kraut's front door.

PING!!! PING!!! PING!!! PONG!!!

What a sweet, metallic sound.

Then the next kid hit the German's mark and the next, and finally I took my toss and hit a *Bullauge,* or bull's eye.

And that's when Kraut himself appeared at the front door and yelled: "You kids come here right now!"

Everybody split but me.

Me, I cowered behind the mail-storage box and hoped the old fireman wouldn't see me.

But he sure did, and he called: "You behind the mail box. You come here! @#$-&*$## kid. I haf called police. You come here right now and wait for ze police to come and put you in the Audy Home where you belong."

The Audy Home was what we called that dreaded dungeon where Cook County sent juvenile delinquents to fester and rot. None of us had yet been to the Audy Home, but all of us had heard the urban legends of the day concerning the horrors visited on bad kids by even badder kids and evil guards at the Audy Home.

If there was a hell on earth, it was the Audy Home, and all any adult or person in authority had to do was threatened to send us to the Audy Home if we didn't straighten up that very second, and we would straighten up that very second.

So, of course, I gave myself up.

I came out from behind the mail-storage box with my hands up and surrendered to the Kraut.

He was lean and mean and grizzled and salty, and he wore suspenders and he seized my arm with iron force, and he told me that he had called the police, and he said he was going to hold me on his front stoop until they came and hauled me off to the Audy Home.

Why, you ask, didn't I kick him in the nuts and run away?

Good question.

And my only explanation is that I was scared out of my wits.

And so I allowed myself to be forced into a sitting position by our neighborhood *Scrooge/Boogeyman/Monster/Kraut*.

I listened to him rant in his accented English about how they were going to set me straight at the Audy Home as I watched my buddies watch me from their hiding places around the intersection.

Cowards.

Why weren't they going to come and rescue me from the German POW camp? I was in the hands of an evil Gestapo interrogator, and--

Then I noticed that a man down the block was looking at us.

He had been out working in his front yard, and he had heard the commotion, and so he was seeing for himself just what was what.

Clearly Mr. Rich, Mr. Donald Rich, didn't like what he was seeing because now he was marching our way.

And, in no time flat, Mr. Rich was right there staring down at the old fireman and demanding to know why he had taken a neighborhood kid captive.

Kraut held me all the tighter and said I was the leader of a gang of hooligans who had attacked his house with *rocks* (not pebbles) and that he was holding me until the police arrived and hauled me off to the Audy Home where I belonged.

Mr. Rich asked me if the old fireman was hurting me, and I just cried.

That's right: I just cried.

I'm surprised I didn't pee in my pants.

Maybe I did.

I know I was so upset that I couldn't talk.

The best speech pathologist in the world couldn't have gotten a peep out of me at that moment.

And then, incredibly, Mr. Rich, Mr. Donald Rich, quick-marched on east to our house at 1645 W. 106th Street and went to the front door.

In a flash there he was on the front porch with my father, pointing down the block to the northwest corner of 106th and Drew and explaining what was what.

Mr. Rich wasn't halfway through when Dad charged to my rescue.

And I do mean charge.

At that moment, I knew exactly how the 101st Airborne felt at Bastogne when the skies cleared and the Mustangs came roaring in out of the blue to blast the Panzers to smithereens.

The 7th Cavalry was galloping to my rescue in the form of my Dad.

Yeah, some of my pals had kidded me about his operation. Yeah, they insinuated not so slyly that my Old Man was less a man for having had his throat sliced and diced.

And I know they were watching him as he stormed west along the sidewalk to the old fireman's house at Drew.

The old fireman asked me if that was my father coming.

"Yes," I said.

"Good," he said. "I tell him what a bad boy you are, and he punish you after the police get through with you."

But that's not how it went down.

No way.

What happened is that Kraut rose with me as Dad approached and began to explain why he was holding me when Dad just hauled off and slugged him in the jaw and sent him falling on his bony, old ass and freeing me.

Dad took me by the hand, and with that golden voice box of his, told me that he was taking me home to await the arrival of the police.

He told the fallen Kraut to send the police to 1645 W. 106th Street, and then he took me home to await my fate.

It arrived shortly thereafter in the form of a steely-eyed Chicago police officer. He had stopped first at Kraut's to ascertain the nature of the complaint, and Kraut had sent him to our house, and now Dad was out there talking to the officer, and then Dad was turning to me and saying: "This policeman wants to talk to you."

That policeman talked to me all right, and the first thing he said was what a terrific father I had.

A Man's a Man for a' that.

And then he told me that I wasn't going to the Audy Home this time.

But next time—

I looked at my Dad and told the policeman there wouldn't be a next time.

And, thanks to Dad, there wasn't.

Chapter Twelve: The Second Landing

You may recall from Chapter Two that our staircase had two landings, and that the second landing faced the living room. Excuse me, it faced *Mac's Bar & Grill*.

This chapter will end on the second landing, but it begins on the first landing where I would sit listening to Dad and Aunt Pudah and Big John and any other guesties Dad had rounded up that night to listen to the music from the good-old days.

Meaning, of course, the Big Band Era.

Meaning, of course, the music of World War II.

Meaning, of course, that nothing good had been written or recorded after 1945.

In fact, according to Dad, nothing good had happened after 1945.

Meaning, of course, that we who were born after 1945 were just no good.

So, of course, we were expected to be seen and not heard and to absolutely respect *grown-up time*, and police the lawn, and help Aunt Pudah across the street, and greet the guesties, and stock the bar, and empty the ashtrays, and light the cigarettes, and then get out of Dodge.

And by *out of Dodge* I do mean the first landing, where I would sit and listen to Dad and the guesties listen to their music.

Meaning mainly Benny Goodman.

Dad dug Benny Goodman so deeply that he was given to say: "That Jew can really play the licorice stick."

Sorry, we were not the Palace of Political Correctness when I was growing up.

There was Dad's blatant anti-Semitism—and Mom's, too— and Big John's fondness for saying: "Come here, kid, and let me show you what we do to the *shines* on the West Side." Then Big John would twist our arms into pretzels and have a good laugh while Dad looked on and had a good laugh. Hey, we were good practice for the *shines* on the West Side.

As for Aunt Pudah, why she just dreamed of a white Christmas, a truly white Christmas.

Like I said, there was no political correctness preached in *Mac's Bar & Grill,* but then you could have gone to any living room in the neighborhood at the time and probably heard pretty much the same guff.

Yeah, guff.

A word Dad used a lot, as in: "Don't give me your guff."

Or: "I wouldn't take any guff from him."

And now back to Benny:

So, Benny Goodman was the musician of choice at *Mac's Bar & Grill,* and Dad and his friends held him and his licorice stick in such high esteem that I decided right then and there on the first landing that I would somehow get a clarinet, learn to play it, and then perform for Dad and the guesties on the second landing.

And they would like me as much as they liked Benny Goodman, and life would be good and sweet and—

Sorry to say, but it didn't work that way.

But, I am happy to say, I did take my request to Mom, and she acted at once and asked around the neighborhood for used clarinets, and sure enough, some friends over on Vanderpoel Avenue had an instrument one of their children no longer used, and next thing I knew I had me a licorice stick and a teacher who was soon telling me that I was hopeless and that I was never, ever going to learn the difference between quarter and eighth notes, and some kids down the block who threw snowballs at me whenever I walked by their house with my clarinet case, and—

Well, I persisted in spite of overwhelming odds.

I practiced in the basement before Dad got home, and I really thought I was going to supplant Benny Goodman at *Mac's Bar & Grill.* What can I say: I was totally delusional.

Mom was encouraging and told me to keep at it, but she advised against practicing while Dad was home. She didn't think I was ready for the big time at *Mac's Bar & Grill.*

But then one night she said I was.

That was the night when she had simply had enough.

Mom just wanted to have a normal family life for once and serve family dinners in the dining room and have peace and quiet in the living room and be done with Aunt Pudah and Big John and the guesties and loud, boorish behavior and—

So she said to me that fateful night when she was hanging by her last thread of sanity: "Go get your clarinet and play for the guesties."

My big moment had arrived.

I was going to show that old Benny Goodman who could really play the licorice stick.

So I went and got my clarinet and appeared on the second landing, and Mom announced to the guesties: "Charley is going to give you a clarinet concert."

And before I was halfway through my first big number—*Twinkle, Twinkle Little Star*—I noticed that all the guesties, even Big John and Aunt Pudah, were stampeding out the front door.

Dad was furious, and I was sent to my room to skulk with my brother who had the good sense to hide away up there.

We could hear Dad having it out with Mom downstairs because that voice box of his, that electrolarynx, carried throughout the house. There was no escaping it.

And there was no escaping the wrath of Dad that night.

I had not supplanted Benny Goodman.

I had failed.

And, a short time later, when the kids down the block hit my clarinet case with ice balls and broke it open and caused my clarinet to crack itself on the frozen sidewalk, why I abandoned the licorice stick and went back to listening to Benny Goodman and dreaming that I would one day play like him.

Yes, Benny Goodman and the guesties returned to *Mac's Bar & Grill* the very next night, but, I am happy to report, I returned to the clarinet at age 58 and have been striving mightily to play some Benny Goodman tunes by my 66th birthday.

Chapter Thirteen: The Sporting Life

The highest compliment Dad could pay someone was to say: "She's a real sport."

By *sport*, he meant that the wife of a drinking buddy went along with the drill. A *sport* didn't complain, or leave, or go to Alanon meetings; a *sport* filled the ice bucket and emptied the ashtrays and greeted the guesties without comment or complaint.

A *sport* didn't have her kid play off-key clarinet on the second landing and drive all the guesties out of *Mac's Bar & Grill*.

Dad obviously didn't consider Mom a *sport* that night.

No siree, Bob.

Dad was a laryngectomee after all, and he had undergone a disfiguring operation that had deprived him of his natural voice, and he was going to recover in the comfort of his own living room, thank you very much, and the least Mom could do was be a *sport* about it, and the least we three McKelvy *bairn* could do was be seen and not heard, and certainly not heard to honk and screech away on the second landing hoping for all the world that we sounded like Benny Goodman.

I obviously didn't sound like Benny Goodman that night, and I probably never will, but I am enjoying the clarinet today, and I am playing it to please myself and no one else.

Although, I must say that when I am toodling away, I sometimes sneak a glance heavenward and think: *What do you think, Daddy-O?*

I like to think that he is in a better place than *Mac's Bar & Grill* and that he smiles down on me from heaven, along, of course, with Benny Goodman.

They're *sports:* my old man and Benny Goodman.

Sports with wings.

And I pray that the two of them are enjoying baseball games without end between the Angels and Saints, and I do offer thanks for the golden sporting moments Dad shared with us while he was with us here on earth where even baseball games do end eventually.

A proud graduate of Penn State, Dad loved to watch and listen to the Nittany Lions tackle opponents on the gridiron, and he loved nothing better than to watch "the golf" on TV as he shined the family's shoes on a Saturday afternoon, but Dad's first love in sports was, and still is, baseball.

And being a transplant to Chicago from Pennsylvania, Dad saw no reason not to cheer for both Chicago teams—the White Sox and the Cubs.

And he did, indeed, take us to see both the White Sox and the Cubs: at Comiskey Park at 35th and Shields and Wrigley Field at Clark and Addison, respectively.

Dad didn't buy that guff that South Siders could only cheer for the White Sox. He said that if a ball team had *Chicago* as its first name, why then he was going to root for that team.

So Dad taught us at early ages to be both White Sox and Cubs fans.

He took us to night games at Comiskey Park where we got to see the likes of Sox lefty Billy Pierce take on Yankees southpaw Whitey Ford, and he loved to haul us on up to the North Side for Cubs day-games against such National League rivals as the Saint Louis Cardinals.

Thanks to Dad, we cheered for shortstops "Little" Luis Aparicio and Ernie "Mr. Cubs" Banks with equal fervor, and thanks to Dad we know how to step up to the troughs at either ballpark and tap our kidneys and hang out with the really *big* guys.

Dad was himself at the old ballpark.

He was Mister Baseball at old Comiskey and Wrigley Field, and he was not self-conscious in either ballpark about speaking with his voice box, with his electrolarynx.

I can picture Dad in his shirtsleeves sitting in a box seat on the first baseline at Wrigley Field, basking in the sun and ordering a beer from the beer man and shucking peanuts and just having a great time at the old ballgame.

We paid to go to Cubs games, but sometimes we got to see Sox games compliments of General Refractories Co. because the sales office bought box seats for customers.

I will always remember that hot summer night in 1959 when the customers couldn't go to the Friday game. Dad said we were going, and he took my brother and me to see the White Sox host the hated New York Yankees in a classic pitchers' duel between the aforementioned Billy Pierce and Whitey Ford.

Dad told us we were going to experience baseball at its best that night complete with an overexcited Sox fan dousing Yankees manager Casey Stengel with beer and that heady aroma of the day's slaughter at the nearby Union Stockyards commingling with spilled beer, overcooked hot dogs, and good, honest body odor.

Oh, my Papa, he was so wonderful when he was at the ballpark.

That's where I remember him best—at the old ballpark.

Especially at Comiskey Park that night in 1959 when the White Sox beat Mickey Mantle and Moose Skowron and Roger Maris and Whitey Ford in as good a ballgame as one could hope to see this side of heaven.

Dad told us to stay close to him all night, and we did, and we shared his unbridled enthusiasm for the greatest game ever invented.

And when Dad took us out front on 106th Street and taught us how to throw and catch with the brand-new Rawlings or Wilson mitts he bought us, we delighted in playing catch with our Dad. We showed the neighborhood that our Dad was the only father on the block willing to go out on the street with his boys and throw the old horsehide around in the twilight of a summer day.

Dad always told us to keep our eyes on the ball.

And we did.

And when Dad took us to see the Blackhawks take the ice at the Stadium on West Madison against the Red Wings, Bruins, Rangers, Maple Leafs, or Canadiens, he always pointed out that Bobby Hull and his teammates were successful because they kept their sticks on the ice. And when he came to watch us play hockey at the rink he helped the men of the neighborhood produce every winter in the Bartlett's big backyard, he insisted that we keep our sticks on the ice.

Dad couldn't swim anymore because of the stoma, or opening, in his neck, but he spent lots of time demonstrating technique on dry land. He told us to relax in the water and to always respect the ocean, lake, or pool.

Look ahead, he said.

Eyes forward.

Crawl through the water.

Keep your eyes on the ball and your stick on the ice.

And: *Be a sport.*

It was hard not to be, especially during baseball season when Dad had the game on the radio he kept in the garage when we were out doing chores with him and watching him offer his friends a cold Drewrys Beer and rejoicing when Ernie Banks hit another homerun.

We loved hockey and football and golf at 1645 W. 106th Street, but we held baseball in the highest esteem, and were grateful to live in a city that offered two—not one, but two—teams to cheer for.

And when the White Sox were American League Champs in 1959 and faced the Los Angeles Dodgers in the World Series, Dad took the week off from work and encamped next door at Big John's house and told us to run home from school at lunch for some ballpark franks and peanuts and the early innings, and then sprint back after the final bell at 3:15 to catch the final innings of those six, heart-breaking games.

Yeah, the Sox lost the series 4 games to 2, but they did beat Sandy Koufax one/zip in game 5, and they looked good for a while in game 6 with Ted Kluszewski's 3-run homer in the 4th, but Don Sherry checked our Sox and took the Dodgers to a 9-3 win and a World Series Championship, and we were there with Dad and Big John just drinking it all in.

Well, they were drinking it all in, and we were drinking pop from the bottle and basking in baseball.

Dad got to see the Cubs come close in 1984 when they jumped two games up on the San Diego Padres in the battle for the National League Pennant before losing three straight, but he died on September 13, 1985 before either of his beloved Chicago baseball teams could win a World Series for him.

So I like to think that the White Sox did it for my Dad 20 years later when they took it all in 2005.

Fans credit Ozzie Guillén with managing the Sox triumph in '05, but we McKelvy children know it was all Dad's doing.

Chapter Fourteen: Christmas & Easter Man

Dad was a *Christmas & Easter Man*, which meant he only went to church with us on Christmas and Easter.

And by church, I do mean the (Protestant Episcopal) Church of the Mediator at 110th and Hoyne, up the hill from Longwood Drive. Our Catholic friends—and we had lots and lots and lots of Catholic friends since we lived in a predominantly Irish-Catholic neighborhood—referred to our church, if they referred to it all, as: *the Church of the Radiator*.

Get it? Radiator, not Mediator.

Anyway, Mom took us to Mediator every Sunday and took a lot of guff for it from Dad who complained that Mediator was "too high-church."

It was, in his view, nothing like All Saints' Episcopal back there on the Mainline of Philadelphia in Wynnewood, Pennsylvania where he and Mom were married on September 2, 1949 and where the priest he referred to as "Doctor Bell" presided over a properly Protestant Episcopal Church. Dad meant the Reverend Doctor Gibson Bell, the man who presided at their marriage in 1949 and the priest who baptized both my brother Donald and me, in 1953 and 1951 respectively.

"Doctor Bell didn't go in for smells and bells," Dad would always say when Mom inevitably tried to get him to up his church attendance.

Dad would go to Mediator with us on Christmas Eve, and he would join us on Easter Sunday, and he would be furious for days afterwards about how we were pretending to be Catholic when we were really a Protestant church that had only added the Catholic trappings late in the 19th century at the instigation of some disaffected English clerics who wanted to drift back to Rome without going all the way back to Rome.

If we were going to worship like Catholics, Dad said, then we should just go to Saint Barnabas Catholic Church at 101st Place and Longwood with our Catholic pals.

But he wasn't about to join us.

And he only went on Christmas and Easter because he said that was what any self-respecting Episcopalian would do.

46

Dad did like the rector who welcomed us to Mediator when we moved to Beverly in 1956: the Reverend Edward Storey.

And, I do remember Dad referring to the man as "Father Storey."

That was huge for Dad, and if he was at ease with the term, that was because Father Storey came to see Dad at home before and after his operation, and because he did such a fine job of baptizing our little Baby Mary. Father Storey furthered his cause by gladly accepting a drink or two when he came to see us.

But Dad didn't like Father Storey enough to attend with us every Sunday.

And he really didn't like the upward liturgical drift Mediator took after Father Storey retired and left the church in the care of a series of high churchmen.

Mom tried to explain that the Diocese of Chicago tended to be a high-church diocese and that Mediator was just a product of its environment, but Dad would have none of it.

He would make himself a Bloody Mary on Sunday morning and loudly complain that "Doctor Bell wouldn't have communion every Sunday," and "Doctor Bell wouldn't wear those Catholic vestments," and "Doctor Bell wouldn't cross himself," and on and on, ad infinitum.

Face it, Dad was not cut out for going to church on a weekly basis, and he had found the perfect excuse for his absence in what he considered the prissy liturgical practices of our priests at Mediator.

Mom always countered by saying: "Jimmy, if you don't like the way we worship at Mediator, find another church that suits you, and we'll go to it with you."

Dad never found another church because he never bothered to look.

I think he liked the order of things.

Church was woman's work.

Sitting in your bathrobe and slippers at home with the Sunday paper and a fresh Bloody Mary on Sunday morning was man's work.

And ne'er the twain should meet, except on Christmas Eve and Easter Sunday, and, oh, yes, for the christening and confirmation of the children and the occasional marriage of friends of the family.

But, you know, we didn't really mind that Dad did not attend church with us on a weekly basis.

Not because we were embarrassed by his voice box and coughing through his stoma.

No, we had learned to live with that.

We were cool with our Dad the Laryngectomee.

Come on, who else had an old man who could make little kids laugh when he buzzed them with his voice box?

Oh yeah, little kids loved Dad, and he loved them.

In fact, I just had this brainstorm that maybe Dad would have been a whole lot happier had he decided after his operation to become a first-grade teacher.

Kids loved him, and he loved them, and that would have been a great way for him to share his considerable knowledge of history and literature, but that was not to be.

Oh well.

We shall not regret the past nor wish to shut the door on it, right?

Right on!

So, there we were back in the 1950s and 1960s with a Dad who wouldn't go to church, except on Christmas Eve, Easter Sunday, and for christening and confirmation of his children.

We didn't mind, not one bit.

That was because of the way in which Dad behaved when he did accompany us to Mediator, which is to say that he would fortify himself with more liquid courage than necessary before he darkened the door of the old church on the hill. Dad was a binge drinker who drank between binges, and he saved his biggest binges for Christmas.

Not so much Easter, because Easter was all about flowers and the resurrection and spring and such, but Christmas brought out Dad's dark side, and he would come home on Christmas Eve with a poinsettia for Mom and a *snootful* of booze for all of us.

And I do mean *snootful*.

Maybe Dad got so loaded on Christmas Eve because he dreaded the prospect of going to church with us later that night.

He clearly hated it, and he clearly let us know every Christmas Eve how much he hated being in church with us, and how he totally disapproved of everything that was happening up there at the altar because it was nothing—absolutely nothing—like the way Doctor Bell did it.

Dad made us miserable the few times he did go to church with us, and so we were happy—thrilled even—that he was a self-avowed *Christmas & Easter Man*.

Good for him, and good for us, except on Christmas and Easter.

But don't think that doesn't mean I don't pray for the Old Man every day.

I do, because, as we used to sing around the old neighborhood back in the day: *Pray for the dead, and they will pray for you.*

In fact, I sponsored a Mass for both Mom and Dad this very morning at Saint Agnes Catholic Church in Sawyer, Michigan.

What, you say, *a Catholic Church?!?*

All will be revealed in its proper order, but suffice it to say I prayed for James and Hannah McKelvy, and asked them to pray for me.

They are simply farther along on the journey we all are taking, and I know they are no longer having the high-church/low-church argument because they are in the highest church of all—heaven.

Amen.

I don't know about you, but I sure could use a potty break right about now.

Way too much tea this morning.

So let's take five and come back in a bit for some: *Scouts in Action.*

Chapter Fifteen: The Scouting Life

The Boy Scouts of America were big on the Beverly scene in the late 1950s and early 1960s.

You couldn't go to the Memorial Day parade on Longwood Drive and not notice that the boy scouts had pride of place.

I certainly noticed, and so I certainly wanted to become a boy in khaki green when I turned 13 in 1963.

But there was one little problem: Dad.

As in Dad declaring: "You can't be in the boy scouts if they expect me to be a leader. I am not going to be a scout leader. End of discussion."

The matter had never come up in regards to the cub scouts because the cub scouts never appeared on our family's radar screen. If they were active in the neighborhood, we didn't know about it, and we didn't care to know about it, because my brother Donald and I were busy, with Dad's limited support, participating in the Ridge-Beverly Little League as members of the Redlegs.

Dad didn't have to coach or help the Redlegs in any way. He only had to go to an occasional game over at Jimmy Murphy Field at 115th Street and the Rock Island tracks. And, of course, he loved sharpening us up for our big games by playing catch with us out on 106th Street and ever reminding us to keep our eyes on the ball.

Little League was fine with Dad, but the boy scouts were going to be a big, big problem if they expected him to have to do anything—anything at all—in the way of leadership and involvement.

Dad made it perfectly clear that he had been disabled by his surgery and that he could not function like other fathers.

So no boy scouts for Yours Truly, or little Donald, who would follow along in just a few years when he turned 13.

End of discussion.

Well, not quite, for Dad's declaration was not the end of scouting at 1645 W. 106th Street.

Not by a long shot.

Mom rolled up her sleeves and worked the phone and found out that the nearest boy scout unit, Troop 607, met on Wednesday nights within walking distance at Bethany Union Church at 103rd and Wood. She sent me over there on a Wednesday night and told me to ask the scoutmaster, the revered Gerry Blake, if membership in the troop was contingent on the willingness of a boy's father to serve as a leader.

You know, I am just starting to wonder if Dad didn't want to be a boy scout when he was a lad and was thwarted by his own father, Eugene Adams McKelvy. Hmm.

Anyway, Gerry Blake said quite simply: "Absolutely not. We would love to have your father get involved, but we do not require it." And then he asked me why my father didn't want to serve.

"He's a laryngectomee," I said, explaining everything. "He can't."

"Fine," Scoutmaster Blake said.

And it was fine with Dad, and even finer with me when I reported for my first meeting.

There was Scoutmaster Gerry Blake in his boy scout uniform standing by the piano at the end of the church hall where Troop 607 met. He had various pertinent papers and forms neatly arranged on the piano top, and he was calmly and quietly in command of a troop of boy scouts that was presently being put through its paces by a senior patrol leader who thought he was a drill instructor at Marine Corps Recruit Depot Parris Island.

I was frightened, but I wanted in. I wanted to be one of those boys in a smart khaki-green uniform with the troop's distinctive orange neckerchief.

Standing at attention.

Marching on command.

Halting on command.

Tying half hitches and square knots on command.

I wanted to be that boy, and I couldn't wait to get my uniform and have my Mom sew all the patches on it, and go camping, and canoeing, and hiking through the forest preserves, and—

I looked past the scoutmaster and realized that I had not noticed another man standing there at the piano. He had obviously just come from work because he was wearing a business suit. He was also wearing a fitted crutch on each arm, and he was leaning on them because he was, as we knew only too well in those days, a victim of that dreaded disease we all called *polio.*

I was stunned and asked the nearest scout who that bent-over man was.

"Oh," he said, "that's Mr. Winkler. He helps out with the merit badges and stuff. He's really cool. You'll like him."

"Yeah, but he's got polio. He's—"

"So?"

So there he was on his crutches at the troop meeting doing what he could do to help.

And my Dad?

My Dad was back at *Mac's Bar & Grill*, doing what he could do to help Aunt Pudah and Big John and the guesties feel like members of his troop.

Chapter Sixteen: The Elephant in the Living Room

By now you're probably wondering why no one said: "Enough is enough. Go to A.A., or we're leaving."

Well, Mom did threaten to go to Alanon.

But she only threatened; she never actually went to a meeting.

I did advise her to go, and, at one point, she threatened to take our sister Mary and leave Dad with his two boys who were turning out just like him.

Oh yeah, we took to the bottle as though it were our birthright.

It was, wasn't it?

Sure it was.

But I get ahead of myself, just a tad.

We noticed that Dad was not your normal social drinker.

We noticed nightly when he went to the picture window and lifted his glass, setting another round of alcoholic chaos into motion.

It was all we could do not to get stepped on by that elephant in our living room.

And, yes, it did smell like peanuts in our living room, or nuts at least, because Dad always insisted on having a bowl of mixed nuts present for the pleasure of his guesties.

Alcoholism is a family disease, and it certainly affects the whole family. We were as affected as any bunch of loonies in the bin. No question about it.

The question was:

What were we to do?

Well, I remember hearing the scuttlebutt at scout meetings that those drunks—those losers from Alcoholics Anonymous—met in a room down the hall from our troop meeting on Wednesday night.

Really?

Oh yeah, really!

So one Wednesday night I slipped away from whatever scout skill we were practicing and went to that room where the drunks met and peered in.

And this is what I saw:

Smoke.

Lots and lots and lots of smoke.

And this is what I smelled, in addition to the cigarette smoke:

Coffee.

Lots and lots and lots of killer coffee.

But I didn't see a single bottle.

And I didn't smell a drop of booze.

Not a one.

And what I heard was:

HOPE.

Not the town in Arkansas, but the virtue that the ancient Greeks despised.

Those men, and they seemed to be mostly men, those men had hope.

They were not drunk, and they hoped they could get through the rest of the day without taking a drink, and, if the Good Lord granted them another day on the morrow, then they planned to ask that *Power Greater Than Themselves* to prevent them from taking that first drink.

All we have is today, they were saying.

Yesterday is history, and tomorrow is a mystery, and all we have is today.

And what a day that was when I looked in on my very first meeting of Alcoholics Anonymous, at, oh say, 14 years of age.

I remember that those A.A. members all stopped talking and looked at me.

I'm sure it was a closed meeting, but I'm also sure they were happy to suspend their sharing to hear me out.

I stood there and wanted to pour out my heart and beg them to head right over to 1645 W. 106th Street and kidnap my Daddy and force him to quit drinking and to join them in their smoke-filled room where there wasn't a single drop of booze.

Not one *snootful.*

But I didn't say a word.

I just stood there and prayed.

And then I went back to my patrol, Eagle Patrol, to continue honing my scout skills.

A scout, after all, is reverent, right?

You bet: it's the penultimate scout law.

Number 12 of 12.

So, yeah, I prayed that night.

And, wouldn't you know, my prayer was answered.

God always says:

a. Yes

b. No

c. Not now.

My name starts with "C" so you know which one I won.

Mac's Bar & Grill was open when I got home from the boy scout meeting that night, and it remained open for decades thereafter.

But my prayer at the door of that A.A. meeting back in 1964 did not end up in the *dead-letter box.*

I should hope not.

And you should not lose hope that I will tell you how and when my prayer for relief from the scourge of active alcoholism was answered.

Chapter Seventeen: The Family Afterward

So we simply learned to live with *the elephant in the living* room and to feed it mixed nuts and freshen its drinks and empty its ashtrays.

We came to accept the double-whammy of cancer AND alcoholism.

What choice did we have?

Well, Mom had threatened to leave with her daughter, our little sister Mary Louise.

But she didn't. She stayed, and we prevailed.

Or coped.

And we developed successful strategies for living with *the elephant in the living room.*

We were careful to avoid any group or club that required a father's participation or that met in members' homes.

Uh uh!!!

Our home was booked exclusively for *Mac's Bar & Grill.*

No, that's not entirely true, for Mom did host bridge club in the living room, during the day, when Dad was decidedly not home.

When he was home, it was his castle, and he was the Lord of the Manor, and we were his servants who were to be seen and not heard.

If we wanted to join a group that met in members' homes then we had to explain that our home was never, ever, never available.

We were remodeling.

There had been a gas leak.

We were having the living room repainted.

The foundation was cracked.

Our house at 1645 W. 106th Street was not available.

Although, I must say, Mom got Dad to agree to allow me to hold my patrol meetings in the basement so long as we didn't interrupt the proceedings upstairs in *Mac's Bar & Grill.* No problem: I had members of Eagle Patrol come in through the side door, totally avoiding the active alcoholism in the living room.

Mom, of course, stepped in where Dad had stepped out. She drove us to overnights way, way out beyond Joliet and drove back in the rain and came back on Sunday to get us. Mom totally helped out with our annual Scout Show in the spring, and she took us to church every Sunday, and she was the sole adult from our house who was active in the PTA.

That's how we coped: we counted on Mom to be both Mom and Dad.

Our Dad couldn't fulfill the duties of fatherhood because he had cancer.

He was a laryngectomee.

That excuse worked more times than it didn't.

I remember the parents of a girlfriend telling me that they perfectly understood that my father drank as he did because he was a laryngectomee.

You would drink, too, if you were a laryngectomee.

I heard that a lot, and I used it as the rationalization for Dad's failure to report for fatherhood.

Oh well.

I cannot speak for my brother and sister in this matter.

They have their own truth and their own stories and their own memories of the way it was and what happened after Dad lost his larynx to cancer.

Please understand that this is my report from the front.

I am writing under my byline.

I speak for no one else.

But I speak from my gut.

And that's where this book resided for decades.

And it was from the gut that the book gushed forth that day the hygienist at the dentist's office asked me what I was writing. She said she had enjoyed reading my work in the local newspapers and missed seeing me in print. She wondered if I was working on anything special or new.

I just said that I was pouring my literary ardor into my blog: www.charleymckelvy.wordpress.com.

"I blog every day," I said.

And she said she would check out my blog, but she clearly wanted more. She wanted me to write again.

Her words stuck to my ribs, and I was not even halfway home from the dentist's office when I stopped in the middle of the blueberry patch and wrote the title and opening lines in my pocket notebook.

A muse had appeared unexpectedly and:

Ding!!!

Start writing, boy.

And, boy, have I ever.

This book has been pouring out of me ever since I started writing it, only a month ago.

This is the book I have always meant to write, and now, as I consider *The Family Afterward*, I realize that I could easily go to a meeting for those with *PTSD*, or *Post Traumatic Stress Disorder*, and qualify for membership.

The only requirement for membership is a desire to get better.

And I am getting better, a word at a time, by writing this book.

So:

The Family Afterward.

Yes, we **WERE** a family afterward.

We stuck it out.

We didn't quit.

We didn't run away.

And, yes, I followed in Dad's footsteps to his corner of the kitchen where the hooch was kept.

But that was when I was 17.

Before then, well, we each had his or her way of coping. As for me, it was what I call *the two B's.* As in:

Bicycles & Books.

More on that in a moment, but first I have to read a good book while I ride the bicycle/trainer.

Chapter Eighteen: Bicycles & Books

Yeah, baby: bicycles & books.

Or, books & bikes.

Say it loud and say it proud(ly):

BIKES & BOOKS.

Bikes & books kept me in the game of living with cancer and active alcoholism.

When the going got too tough for this little shaver, he would hop on his Schwinn bicycle—was there any other brand?—and ride over to the Walker Branch of the Chicago Public Library at 111th and Hoyne where he would take that magic-carpet ride that only books can provide.

Books were my balm of Gilead.

My comfort.

My joy.

My solace.

My sanity.

Were it not for my trusty Schwinn and that repository of literature at the top of the hill on 111th Street at Hoyne we fondly called *the Walker Branch*, I would have gone mad.

Absolutely mad.

Of that I am quite certain.

I had no support group.

No sympathetic therapist.

No intervening child-protection agency.

None of that.

Just suck up the cancer and ignore *the elephant in the living room* and keep those drinks fresh and those ashtrays empty.

Deal with it, Sonny Boy!

So I did.

In my own way.

And, as I said, the way to mental health was simple: *bikes & books.*

So how did it work for me?

Case in point:

One night, when I could take no more and was so full of adrenalin that I feared for my father's safety, I went out to the garage, hopped on my black Schwinn with coaster brakes, and rode off into the night pretending to be that RAF fighter pilot I had just read about in a book I had borrowed from the Walker Branch.

I rode to the end of 106th Street, turned north on Wood Street, and kept on riding until I found myself riding the trails of the Dan Ryan Woods Forest Preserve at 87th and Western, a good two miles northwest of my house.

Sealed in the cockpit of my make-believe *Spitfire*, I shot down one German bomber after another, defending my homeland in the dark.

I was a stealth fighter before there were stealth fighters, and I flew through the dark with the wind in my face and hope in my heart.

If I could be like the characters in the novels and stories of my literary pushers—Mark Twain, James Fennimore Cooper, Robert Louis Stevenson, Jack London, H.G. Wells, and even Edgar Allen Poe, why then I could be every bit as brave as Natty Bumppo and Huck Finn.

I could stand up to the Martians and the wild beasts of the Alaskan wilderness and keep my head about me.

So, yeah, books and bicycles.

Or just: *bikes & books*.

And to illustrate just how far along I got on this escape route, let me tell you a true story from the summer of, oh, say 1962 when an actual Catholic was in the White House, and my two best friends in the whole wide world were actual Catholics.

I'm talking about *Casey* and *Bowline* here, and that's all you need to know of their names.

Suffice it to say, we three were inseparable in the summer when we were free of that horrible Catholic/public school separation from September to June. We pal'd around every day, and when it rained we holed up at Casey's house where we would read his father's books about World War II or play such militaristic board games as *Risk, Broadside, Civil War,* or *Stratego*.

We knew everything there was to know—without having been there—about the Bataan Death March and President Kennedy's exploits in the Pacific as the skipper of PT-109. We each built the model and we knew how to torpedo Jap destroyers in the dark.

Casey and *Bowline* knew what I was up against at my house, so we did most of our playing there in the backyard. Best to keep it outside when *Mac's Bar & Grill* was in session inside.

So one golden summer day we decided to pretend that we were joining Captain Meriwether Lewis and Second Lieutenant William Clark on their 1804-06 expedition to establish an American presence from sea to shining sea.

President Thomas Jefferson wanted us to go west with Lewis and Clark, and we answered the call that late June day and mounted our Schwinns and rode to Wood, and then to Prospect, and then to 111th Street, and then all the way west past Worth to Palos Hills and the Cal-Sag Channel and Saganashkee Slough, and finally to our ultimate objective: the Forest Preserve District of Cook County's toboggan slides at Swallow Cliff.

We ran silent, and we rode deep, and we had no maps or spare tires or any money to speak of. We were just three boys off on an adventure with absolutely no parental knowledge or approval.

We had pretty much decided by that point that the adult was an animal not to be trusted.

So we took flight on our Schwinns, and, yes, we made it to the foot of those daunting toboggan slides that we had shushed down so many times in winter, and we dared one another to push our clunky bikes to the top and ride down.

Crazy, right?

Oh yeah.

Nuts as they come.

That we were: *the Apache Runner, Casey,* and *Bowline.*

Yes, I was *the Apache Runner.*

Casey and *Bowline* tagged me *the Apache Runner* because although I could never catch them on foot, I never stopped trying. They were faster by far, but I was more persistent by far.

Just like an Apache runner.

So I was *the Apache Runner,* and there I was at the summit of the Palos toboggan slides with my best buddies, *Casey* and *Bowline.*

We looked down that mountain of wintry pleasure that was woodenly reflecting the summer sun, and chorused: "Last one to the bottom's a rotten egg."

I don't know who the rotten egg was that day, but oh boy, did we boys have fun.

We didn't fall or fail or get hurt or have a flat on the long, long ride home.

And we didn't tell a soul what we had done that day.

When our moms asked what we had done that day, we just said we had done what we always did in summer: "Went bike ridin'."

That's what we did.

Bike ridin'.

And books.

And that's what kept me afloat: ***Bikes & Books.***

Thank you, very much, both: ***Bikes & Books.***

Chapter Nineteen: Fast Forward

With your permission, we are going to fast forward here to an afternoon in the spring of 1967 when I was a junior at Morgan Park High School, which, according to *Wikipedia*, "is a public, 4-year high school and academic center located in the Morgan Park neighborhood on the far-south side of Chicago, Illinois at the intersection of 111th Street and Vincennes Avenue."

And, so as not to confuse you, allow me to explain that the aforementioned *Beverly* neighborhood where we lived extended from 87th Street on the north to 107th Street on the south, and that our sister neighborhood of Morgan Park went from 107th Street to 119th Street where the suburb of Blue Island began.

None of this is important enough to remember, trust me.

You just need to know that I had made it to that day in 1967 in a righteously sober state and that I had spent most of my young life vowing to never turn out like my father.

Which is to say: a drunk.

Let's cut to the chase here.

Despite the title, this book is as much about alcoholism as it is about cancer of the larynx.

Just so we're straight here, okay?

Good. Let's move on:

Through most of my junior year I had been what the greasers at Morgan Park called a *milk & cookie boy.*

Meaning that I was not only clean-cut and serious about my studies and varsity swimming, but that I did not drink or smoke.

I had even gone so far as to join a non-drinking fraternity at Morgan Park: the original *milk & cookie boys*, or Beta Tau Beta. I was a serious young teetotaler, make no mistake about me.

But don't think alcohol had never crossed my lips, because it most certainly had, beginning that summer of 1953 at my grandfather's cottage on Long Beach Island in New Jersey when the grown-ups gave the kid—this kid—a wee dram o' scotch.

Did I like it?

You bet I did.

Love at first sip, and as the grown-ups said: "Hey, the kid likes it."

Of course, I did.

But I didn't like what the booze did to my Daddy and his friends and our family.

Alcoholism is a family disease, and I was a member of one truly diseased family.

But by the middle of my junior year, my roots were showing.

I slip-slided away from the *milk & cookie boys* and finally just resigned from Beta Tau Beta.

The booze was talking to me from my Old Man's liquor cabinet, and I was thinking that if I couldn't beat him I might as well join him.

Sure, I had swum hard my junior year and had shown my coach potential for my senior year. He was convinced I would place at the city meet my senior year in my events: the 100- and 200-yard freestyle.

No problem.

I just had to remain clean, sober, and fit.

But by the spring of 1967 I was ready to come unsprung.

And I did.

Don't ask me why, but I did.

Well, ask me why.

Why?

Because I'm an alcoholic.

That's why.

So one day at school I asked a couple of my buddies if they'd like to head over to my house for "some cocktails."

Oh yeah!

They were all about that, and we were all about to puke in no-time flat because we had had the poor judgment to pour every kind of booze found at *Mac's Bar & Grill* down our throats.

It wasn't pretty.

It never is.

And we were not urbane or sophisticated.

I never was.

I thought I was, but I never made the grade, starting that afternoon in 1967.

As soon as I poured Dad's liquor down my throat that afternoon in 1967 I realized I was merely rekindling the love affair that began that summer evening in 1953 on Long Beach Island when I was three.

I was back in class, and the class was all about eliminating any and all class from my life.

Bring it on!

Oh yeah, baby!

Bring it on!

So I did.

And, to hide our pilfering from the old man, we refilled those bottles of scotch, gin, vodka—and, yes, crème de menthe—with water. I knew he always carefully checked the levels, so I figured it would be easy to trick him.

But when he got home that night and tucked into his first drink, he made a sour face and said: "Who's been watering down my booze?"

I 'fessed up.

Maybe that's why I was meant to become a Catholic in later life: I was good at confessing my sins.

I was out front with what we had done and prepared for the worst, but all I got—and I'll always, always, always remember what I got that night, which was—"If you're going to drink my booze, be a man and drink it. But don't water down good booze."

All righty then!

A man's a man for a' that, and me and my old man were suddenly sailing on the same ship.

More on that in a minute.

Much, much more, but the sun is over the yardarm and it's time for a drink—of water, thank you very much.

Chapter Twenty: Shipmates

As I write this, I am looking at a photograph of Utility Squadron Fifteen. I mounted it over my desk so I could gaze daily at the unit that was commissioned 23 June 1943 at U.S. Naval Air Station, Brunswick, Maine to help prosecute *the War in the Atlantic* against the Third Reich's dreaded wolves under the sea, or U-boats. And there in the back row is Lt. (JG) McKelvy. My Dad was by far the most handsome officer in that squadron of dashing men in dress blue. He had already served in the U.S. Marine Corps and U.S. Army by the time he earned his commission in the U.S. Navy, and he talked often of his wartime experiences, and we will, too, but first to two other framed objects on my wall:

1. I have only to shift my gaze slightly up and to the left from the black-and-white photograph of Utility Squadron Fifteen to see my Honorable Discharge from the United States Navy Reserve in 1979.

2. And then, if I drop my eyes from my discharge, I see a photograph I took of Honorably Discharged Lieut. Cmdr. James S. McKelvy, U.S.N.R. aboard a U.S. Navy frigate that was visiting Chicago in 1978 as part of a goodwill tour of the Great Lakes.

I have run the thread of my life with my father through these three frames, and I can tell you now that it was the U.S. Navy that brought my father and me together.

We were bound by the Navy from my earliest childhood.

Permit me, if you will, to quote from an article I wrote for *World War II Magazine* in March 2002:

Although Germany surrendered on May 7, 1945, I thought they were still at war with us in September 1954 when I was all of 4 years old and living on the South Side of Chicago. My peculiar belief arose from the fact that my parents and their friends had taken me to the Museum of Science and Industry, where they were in the process of rolling a captured German submarine, U-505, across Lake Shore Drive to its final resting place outside the museum.

I remember hearing my parents and their friends joke about the "Submarine Crossing" sign posted along the drive, and I distinctly recall one of the adults solemnly telling me that "the Germans are invading Chicago, and there are German sailors hiding aboard that U-boat."

Alarmed, I told my parents we had better high-tail it out of there as fast as possible. They laughed and reassured me that their friend had been joking with me, but I was not so sure. In fact, when my wife (Natalie) and I paid a recent visit to the U-505, I looked behind every bulkhead just to be sure the boat was truly free of Marinesoldaten. *Although my return to the submarine was perhaps a little less terrifying than it had been when I was a young boy, I found the museum's account of its capture by a carrier-destroyer task force commanded by Chicagoan Daniel V. Gallery as compelling as ever.*

And I still find it compelling because I know my father and his shipmates in Utility Squadron Fifteen helped make it possible for Captain Gallery's aircraft carrier *Guadalcanal* and accompanying destroyers to cripple the U-505, capture it, and, well, back to my narrative from *World War II:*

According to the museum, Captain Gallery and his task force of six ships on patrol off West Africa hit the jackpot just a month after sailing from Norfolk, Va. On June 4, 1944 (when my Dad was on patrol elsewhere in the Atlantic with Utility Squadron Fifteen), *the destroyer escort Chatelain made sonar contact with U-505, which in its 404 days of service had become a terror of the sea, sending eight freighters to the bottom.*

And, as an editorial aside, be it known that my father saw ships torpedoed by U-boats as he was standing on the beach in Virginia Beach, Virginia. Dad saw, heard, and smelled how real the threat was and how absolutely essential it was that the U.S. Navy launch such effective countermeasures as the carrier-destroyer task forces commanded by the likes of Captain Gallery.

So:

Chatelain fired again and again at the sub as Grumman F4F Wildcat fighters from Captain Gallery's aircraft carrier Guadalcanal circled overhead, marking the sub's position with machine-gun fire. Six and a half minutes after Chatelain's first attack, the U-boat surfaced and her crew surrendered. But the excitement was far from over. The attack had jammed U-505's rudder; the sub was out of control, and the German crew had already jumped into the water. Waves washed over the sub's deck as she slowly began to sink.

The Americans did not know how long U-505 would stay afloat or whether she might be booby-trapped inside. Undaunted, a volunteer boarding part of nine men from USS Pillsbury—only one of whom had ever been in a submarine before—tumbled down the hatch.

Water was pouring in from a 10-inch sea strainer. Thinking quickly, Engineer's Mate Zenon Lukosius searched for the scuttle valve and secured it. For the first time in 129 years, Americans had captured an enemy warship on the high seas.

In capturing U-505, Gallery's men also seized the submarine's addressbuch *(code book), which provided the Allies with the information they needed to keep shipping lanes open in preparation for D-Day, just 48 hours later.*

I share all this because I am so very proud of my father for his role in what he always called *the Battle of the Atlantic.*

He often said that after he became what he called a *ninety-day wonder,* he hoped to serve aboard a ship like Captain Gallery's aircraft carrier *Guadalcanal.*

He joined the Navy to serve at sea.

But the Navy would have him serve above the sea with Utility Squadron Fifteen doing everything that a utility squadron did from 1943 until the war's end in 1945.

Meaning that my Dad and his fellow officers searched for the likes of *U-505* and flew supplies to the Royal Navy in Bermuda and just basically did whatever was needed to open the shipping lanes and keep the materiel flowing to embattled England and Russia.

Thanks, Dad!

If I didn't say it before, I'll say it again:

THANKS, DAD!

So I grew up listening to my Dad talk about his war in the Atlantic and looking at pictures of him in his dress blues with Utility Squadron Fifteen and hearing him sing the praises of Captain Daniel V. Gallery and Winston Churchill and the U.S. Navy in general.

Dad presented the Navy in such a positive light that I positively resolved to follow in his footsteps and serve as an officer in the U.S. Navy after graduation from college.

To that end I took the Naval-ROTC qualification examination during my senior year at Morgan Park. My plan was to earn a NROTC scholarship to Northwestern University where I would major in journalism. I would be commissioned as a naval officer upon graduation, serve my active and reserve duty time in this man's navy, and then work as a reporter for, oh, the *Chicago Tribune* would do.

The self-proclaimed *World's Greatest Newspaper* was what Dad read every morning, so I would report for the *Tribune*, probably as a foreign correspondent in Beirut and Saigon and Moscow and Peking (yeah, Beijing was called Peking in those days before political correctness).

Well, I should have known from the location of the NROTC exam at Illinois Institute of Technology, or IIT, that my bold plan was, as Bobby Burns penned in his ode *To a Mouse*: apt to: *gang aft a-gley.*

I was done with math and science by my senior year and walked into that exam without a slide rule and minus even a rudimentary understanding of ship's navigation.

I took one look at the other applicants and realized that I was a flounder swimming with the sharks.

I am sure they all aced the test and went on to become brilliant naval officers, probably serving in and around the Republic of Vietnam, or South Vietnam.

All I know is that the Navy was not long in informing me that I had failed miserably.

I was no ship driver.

I couldn't navigate my way out of a paper bag.

And then Northwestern dropped the other shoe by curtly informing me that the best I could hope for from them was to be put at the end of an endless waiting list.

Dad said it was time to get real.

Time to pick a state university in Illinois and apply there.

No chance of following in his footsteps to Penn State because the out-of-state tuition was too high.

A state university in Illinois would have to do, and it did: Illinois State University in Normal.

Or, as we fondly referred to it: *Abnormal.*

Illinois State University, ISU if you will, accepted me, and I went there, and Dad loved it.

He loved driving me back to school on old Route 66, and I must say that we had some great times together motoring back and forth between Chicago and Normal on that iconic American highway.

We were very much on the same political page my freshman year of college in 1968-69. So much so that when some recruiters from the U.S. Marine Corps appeared at the student union one gray day, I gladly glad-handed them and took the test they offered to qualify for the Platoon Leader Class, or PLC. They said that if I qualified I would receive intensive training during the summers after my sophomore and junior years and then be commissioned as a second lieutenant in the U.S. Marines upon graduation.

I aced the test that very day, and I was as gung-ho as they come and quite willing to go to Vietnam as a Marine second or first lieutenant.

I bought the whole *Domino Theory* deal and believed that the *Red Horde* would be landing on California beaches in no time flat if we didn't stop Ho Chi Minh and his pals in South Vietnam.

Yeah, baby.

So of course Dear Old Dad and I were on the same political page as he drove me up and down Route 66. We were getting our kicks on 66 all right, but when I broke the news of my acceptance into the Marine Corps officer-training program, he was less than enthused.

Quite a bit less, and then I remember him telling me how he had been in Marine boot camp before he was accepted by the Navy as a candidate for officer training. The drill sergeants were drilling Dad and his fellow recruits for hand-to-hand combat with the Imperial Japanese Army on the islands of the South Pacific.

Remember the name of Captain Gallery's aircraft carrier?

Guadalcanal ring a bell?

Yeah, well, that ship was named for that island where Dad was headed with his fellow Marines before he washed out due to a thyroid deficiency.

I wouldn't be here right now writing this or any other chapter, if Dad's thyroid hadn't gone haywire on him in the early days of America's involvement in World War II.

He was headed for Guadalcanal, and if I have to spell out what it was like to be a U.S. Marine on Guadalcanal in 1942 then you need to take U.S. History again.

Suffice it to say, Dad dodged a whole hive of Jap bullets, and he never forgot that. He was haunted by the fact that his boot-camp buddies had gone to Guadalcanal to meet the Japanese in some of the worst fighting of the campaign to take the island, and he never even considered buying a Japanese car as a result.

Dad seemed to think the Germans were fair fighters because they were fellow Europeans, while he considered the Japs, and he never called them anything better than Japs, to be barbarians, bound by no civilized code of warfare.

And although he didn't say it, I think he feared that the North Vietnamese and Vietcong would do to me, as a freshly minted lieutenant in this man's U.S. Marine Corps, what the Japs would have done to him in the South Pacific.

So Dad did not say much about my enlistment in the Marine PLC program.

He was, now that I think of it, strangely silent.

But his brother-in-law, Booth Mattson, was not.

Uncle Booth had served as an officer in the Marine Corps, and he took great pride in being a Marine, for after all one is always a Marine. He took pride in showing me the sword he had been presented at his commissioning and said it was earned, not given.

So naturally I wanted to earn my own sword, and I wanted so much to share my good Marine Corps news with Uncle Booth that I told him straight away of my exciting news.

Rather than look pleased, Uncle Booth looked alarmed and said: "Can you get out of it?"

"Well, sure, but—"

But nothing.

Uncle Booth had served between the wars in Korea and Vietnam. He had been a peacetime Marine, but he knew what the Marines were up against in South Vietnam. He knew from friends in the Corps how ugly and dangerous and totally deadly it was becoming over there in the jungles of Vietnam.

So he told me to quit, if I could.

And, shortly thereafter, I was at a party in the neighborhood bragging to anyone who would listen about how I was going to be a big, bad-ass Marine officer in Vietnam, and—

A friend who had just returned from serving in Vietnam grabbed me by the shoulder and hauled me outside and hollered in my face: "How long do you think you're going to last over there with that stripe on your helmet?!? If the Vietcong don't shoot you in the face, your men are going to shoot you in the back when you give them some dipshit order to attack some position they can't possibly take."

His advice was the same as Uncle Booth's: quit as soon as you can.

And so I did, eventually.

That was a journey worthy of a separate book, but suffice it to say I changed my thinking about the war in Vietnam and the Domino Theory.

Okay, I was a 19-year-old who didn't want to die, for his country or anyone else.

I didn't want to die, period.

Quite simple, really.

And I am really sorry to say I wasn't able to have that conversation with my father.

When I began to speak out against the war in Vietnam, he spoke all the louder for it.

We argued in the living room and at the local watering hole where we would drink together.

I was a hippie pinko and he was an Archie Bunker redneck warmonger.

Ne'er the twain shall meet.

But it did, eventually.

After my successful attempt to stay out of Vietnam played out at the seminary that had given me a 4D deferment, I enlisted in—you saw this coming miles back—the U.S. Navy.

Yep, if you can't beat 'em, join 'em, and I let that recruiter sweet-talk me into a hitch in this man's Navy over beers and billiards at some gin mill not far from the seminary I was falling out of for lack of funds for tuition and for lack of a real order to holy orders.

My life was a mess, and the Navy was looking good, and when I came home from the Great Lakes Naval Training Center in my dress blues, my old man hugged me so hard my eyeballs are still popping.

So there's your full circle, down to that third picture of him aboard a U.S. Navy frigate in 1978 and looking out to sea.

The sea might have only been Lake Michigan, but it was a sea change for both of us to be on that ship with him a proud veteran of the U.S. Navy and me still serving in the United States Navy Reserve.

And what did we do that fine day after being aboard ship together?

Why we cemented our nautical bond by doing what sailors do the world over: we went and had ourselves copious measures of grog at a public house in the Loop worthy of our salty patronage.

Chapter Twenty-One: Your Dad's Your Dad

Credit the late John Gregory Dunne for coming up with that line, and I recall that I read it in Dunne's wickedly delightful novel of Irish-Catholic assimilation into American culture, *The Red, White and Blue.*

A priest—it's always a priest isn't it—blithely assures the protagonist:

Your dad's your dad.

What the good padre meant to say was that the man just had to suck it up and accept his father for who he was, not what he wanted him to be.

Reading John Gregory Dunne—and I **DO** recommend that you read John Gregory Dunne—helped me accept my father for who he was, which was a flawed human being just like me.

I saw, and see, so much of my father in myself that it scares me.

In fact, when I would get in my cups and start railing against the outrageous fortunes of life and death, my dear wife Natalie would always bring me up short by saying: "You sound just like your father."

OUCH!!!

All right, back to the narrative:

So, yes, the U.S. Navy brought us closer as Dad closed in on his death on September 13, 1985 at the age of 67. And, yes, I told my father I loved him the night he died, at 1645 W. 106th Street. And, yes, I will most certainly devote an entire chapter to our final times together and the journey we took to get there.

But for this chapter, I want to talk about the bad times and the good times I had with my father, the alcoholic laryngectomee.

A particularly bad time was in June 1968 when I was hosting a pre-prom party in our living room—who am I kidding, in *Mac's Bar & Grill*—at good, old 1645 W. 106th Street.

We boys were all turned out in our rented tuxedoes—I was particularly spiffy in my lime green jacket—and our dates were dazzling us with their lovely dresses and elegant coiffures. We boys and girls were men and women in the making that night, and I only agreed to host the pre-prom party because Mom promised me that she would declare the living room a Mac-free zone that night and order my father to work late or stay as long as he liked at the last bar before home.

Mom had nearly succeeded in shutting down *Mac's Bar & Grill* by then, so Dad had been reduced to taking his liquid comfort in the various drinking establishments that met his high standards. Basically, that meant a good bartender who knew how to mix and serve without a lot of guff.

Mom promised that Dad would not embarrass me or my friends.

She said she had gotten him to promise that he would not come home that night until we were all headed downtown for the prom.

Kind of sad, isn't it, that your dad who is your dad, has to stay away from your pre-prom party because he's a raging alcoholic?

Welcome to my childhood.

So that was the deal that night of my gala pre-prom party: Dad would "work" late, and we wouldn't see hide nor hair of him.

But then, as we all stood in my living room sipping our unspiked punch, we saw an all-too-familiar sedan lurch up to the curb in front of my house.

Yep, it was Dear Old Dad coming home earlier than expected from the last bar on his trap line. He had such a snootful that he could not parallel-park the car. In fact, he drove that *Made in America Car* of his up and over the curb, and then he tumbled out of the car, staggered to his feet, and stared angrily at the interlopers in HIS living room.

In *Mac's Bar & Grill*.

It was, after all, cocktail hour.

Time for the guesties to arrive.

Time for children to be seen and not heard, and certainly not the time for boys and girls to pretend they were men and women. And certainly not the time for kids to be drinking kiddie cocktails in *Mac's Bar & Grill*.

"Hey, there's your dad," my date said. "I finally get to meet him."

"Oh no you don't," I muttered as my heart slid down my lower GI tract.

"What?!?"

"Nothing, I—"

I prayed. Oh, did I pray for a miracle. For deliverance from the scourge of active alcoholism. *Please don't let my Daddy stumble in here and make a drunken fool of himself. Please don't let me kill him if he does. Please—*

And then, as pleasing to my sight as a heavenly host of angels, came Aunt Pudah in her fluttering muumuu. She swept across 106th Street, gave Dear Old Dad one of her come-hither looks, and hauled him over to her house to drink the rest of the night away while we kids finished our kiddie cocktails.

That was one of the bad times with Dad. One of the worst.

And it was only redeemed by the timely intervention of my honorary aunt, Pudah.

God bless and keep you, Pudah!

I wished upon a star at that moment that I had a father like my friend Jonathan's father. His dad was a Lutheran minister, and we would go to Jonathan's house on Christmas Eve and marvel at what it was like to live in a household where Dad didn't come home drunk and then erupt at the table about "the dirty little Japs," or his War in the Atlantic, or get all teary-eyed over the war-time speeches of Winston Churchill, which he would quote from memory.

Oh, how I longed for my father to be normal.

To stop drinking.

To give it all up and just be the good father that he could be when he wanted to be.

And he could be a great father when he wanted to be.

He certainly celebrated my achievements in the Navy, and, ironically, in the boy scouts, particularly when I became an Eagle Scout.

Although Dad had not deigned to have anything to do with Troop 607, he did delight in our scouting milestones, and he particularly enjoyed driving up to our summer camp near Whitehall, Michigan for family day.

Dad was your go-to-guy for a road trip, be it to get some kicks on old Route 66, or to head east on the Pennsylvania Turnpike.

Dad became my best drinking buddy, as you shall see in the next chapter, and he was great to be with at all those parades he loved.

No one quite loved a parade as much as my Old Man, and he particularly loved standing at the corner of 107th and Longwood, watching the Memorial Day parade.

He launched me on my Schwinn bicycle in that parade just after we moved to Beverly from South Shore in 1956, and I am looking at a photograph on my desk right now that shows Dad watching me that first tentative ride on my brand-new Schwinn bicycle. Yeah, he had to put on the training wheels because I wasn't ready for the prime time yet, but the look on his face in that picture is priceless. It is the look of a father who has just worked hard to do something great for his kid, and then hopes the kid flies like an eagle.

My brother Donald is looking on with wonder, and I know Dad did more for my brother over the years than can be possibly told in 10 books.

Dad was a great Dad.

When he wanted to be.

That was the problem.

He didn't always want to be.

Still, *Your Dad's your Dad.*

And I do have Dad to thank for the greatest gift of my life.

She would be Natalie, of course, and we will celebrate 38 golden years of marriage on August 13, 2015.

Natalie and I have a wonderful life together, and I have to give Dear Old Dad a fair measure of credit.

We fought, you see, in the summer of 1977 and broke up.

We had been planning to marry, but then we had a huge fight over therapy, and we split up.

Mom was thrilled.

She never liked Natalie, and never really did. Well, she did like to be waited on by Natalie at the end of her life, but that's the subject of my next book.

So when I broke the news to Mom and Dad at *Mac's Bar & Grill*, Mom was thrilled and said: "I never liked her."

But Dad was not happy.

He had greeted Natalie warmly when I first brought her home to meet the family for Christmas in 1976, and he had smiled as he watched us dance at a friend's wedding in Beverly in the spring of 1977.

So when I broke the news about the break-up, Dad took me aside and said: "You were really happy with her. She's the one, Char."

That's right, he called me *Char* when we were having such moments.

"Don't let her go."

I didn't.

I went back to Natalie, and, yes, I went to therapy, and we were happily wed in a lovely ceremony at the First Methodist Church in Evanston, Illinois on Saturday, August 13, 1977.

Dad loved everything about our wedding, particularly the touches he had inspired: a reading from Shakespeare by a friend, and a piper in full dress to skirl us out of the church, and, of course, the well-stocked bar at the reception at Natalie's parents' house. I had personally stocked that bar, and I was careful to provide plenty of Dad's favorite scotch. Also my favorite, wouldn't you know?

It was a magical evening at 235 Clark Drive in Palatine, Illinois, and after my friends and I drained the last keg and sang: *I did it my way,* Dad took me aside and said words to me I will always remember: "You two will be very happy."

John Gregory Dunne got it right when he wrote:

Your dad's your dad.

Chapter Twenty-Two: He Stopped in Time

Do you remember that prayer I uttered back in *Chapter Sixteen: The Elephant in the Living Room?*

As I stood in my boy scout uniform outside that A.A. meeting in 1964, I prayed for deliverance from the scourge of the bottle.

I was thinking that a power greater than myself would relieve my father from his constant need to drink to excess and thus restore our family to sanity.

But my Higher Power, whom I chose (and choose) to call God, had another solution entirely.

Who says God doesn't have a sense of humor?

Right?

I speak from my own experience, so I know I'm right.

At least as far as the grace of God applies to me, and me alone.

So, as I said, Dad and I became great drinking buddies. We loved to drink the trifecta in the Chicago Loop, which consisted of:

1. Binyon's on Plymouth Court,
2. The Berghoff on Adams, and
3. Miller's Pub on Van Buren.

We would drink our way through a liquid luncheon of turtle soup and pot roast at Binyon's, and top it off with strudel and stingers with crème de menthe and brandy poured over crushed ice.

Yum-mee!

Stung by multiple stingers at Binyon's, we would then stagger over to the Berghoff's men's bar (yes, there was a men's bar at the Berghoff once upon a time) for a glass or two of the house suds, and then stumble over to Miller's Pub for a chaser at the bar.

Dad and I got blasted at the old ballgame before, during, and after many a Cubs game at Wrigley Field, and to prepare for Christmas 1981, we hit the trifecta in the Loop.

I came home to our North Side apartment so drunk that Natalie wanted to disown me on the spot.

But I bought time by assuring her that I was merely honoring "an annual family tradition. Just a few drinks with Dear Old Dad, is all."

Don't you know?

Well, Natalie didn't know quite yet, because she gave me one more pass.

But then I passed out the next day after having a *few* Christmas drinks with a friend.

Natalie was nervous and reminded me that I was behaving just like my father.

I assured her that I was simply celebrating Christmas in the fine McKelvy manner, and—

Natalie noted I had been celebrating non-stop since Halloween and wondered: "When are you going to stop?"

"Soon. Any day now. Just as soon as—"

"If this doesn't stop, then this marriage stops."

Uh oh!

I had been served.

But I continued being served at one gin mill after another and even went so far as to show up late and wasted for a movie date with Natalie on the Gold Coast. I had been with one of my dazzling and delightful drinking buddies at a seriously ethnic bar on the far, far South Side, drinking shots of vodka and imported beers and had wondered while I was there why all those sad sacks were drinking their lives away when they should have been home soberly celebrating the Christmas holidays with their families.

Then I looked in the mirror behind the bar and saw that my rosy-cheeked self was exactly one of those sad sacks.

What a load of guff I had been selling myself.

And Natalie.

And the lady who cleaned our apartment.

Yes, one morning in late 1981, I was writing a press release for a business client in my home office when she popped in with her feather duster.

It was close to noon—well, 10:30 is close to noon, right?—so I said: "Want a beer?"

I was having a beer, or two or three, so I figured she should have one, too. A beer was making me more productive at 10:30 in the morning, and it would certainly do the same for her.

She, who will forever remain anonymous, looked like a real party chick, so I was sure she would consent, especially since Natalie was conveniently gone for the day to work at her office in the Loop.

But no, the party chick with the feather duster said: "No thanks. I don't drink anymore."

"What?!?"

"I quit."

"What?!?"

"It wasn't good for me, so I quit."

"Come on, one beer's not gonna kill you. It's almost noon and—"

"I go to those meetings. You know."

Oh yeah, I knew all about *THOSE MEETINGS* from that evening in 1964 when I so much wanted my drunken Daddy to go to *THOSE MEETINGS*. So I swallowed hard and said: "Yeah. Good for you. I hear that really works for some people."

"It sure works for me, and I was a hopeless drunk."

Or words to that effect, and the effect on me was electric.

I was zapped.

Slapped down.

Kidney-punched.

But all I could say was: "Great. Good on you. Say, uh, I, uh, have a friend who drinks too much. I should—"

"Tell him to call me if he wants to stop. I go to some great meetings around here."

"Yeah. Sure. I will."

And then I told her I had to get back to work, and she went off with her feather duster, and I could not—for the life of me—make the rest of that beer on my desk taste any better than day-old pond scum.

Whoops!

I had finally stepped in the stinking pile of my alcoholic insanity.

The God of my understanding, that power greater than myself, had heard my plea for help back in 1964 and sent me a herald angel in 1981 with a solution.

But I wasn't quite ready.

I was, after all, a binge drinker who drank between binges, so I had to run the holiday table.

And so I continued on my merry way into the New Year of 1982.

I was ready to maintain my blistering pace at least until Valentine's Day when Natalie gave me her life-changing ultimatum:

EITHER YOU STOP DRINKING RIGHT NOW, OR I LEAVE. YOUR MARRIAGE OR YOUR DRINK. THE CHOICE IS YOURS. ALL I KNOW IS THAT I HAVE HAD ENOUGH. I CAN'T TAKE IT ANYMORE. UNDERSTOOD?

Only too well, and so I called our cleaning lady that day and asked her when and where the next one of *THOSE MEETINGS* was.

"That friend of yours want to go?" she asked.

"Yeah, you could say that. So—"

So she gave me good, orderly directions to a meeting on January 6, 1982 of men and women who had stopped drinking, one day at a time.

I told Natalie I was going for her, and she told me I should go for myself.

And off I went by myself that bitterly cold January night when the holidays were well and truly over.

But, stop to think of it, January 6th WAS Twelfth Night, and I was looking to join an organization famous for its 12 steps of recovery, and—

I walked into that meeting, which fittingly was held in the classroom of an elementary school, fully expecting to be brainwashed by a bunch of dour cult figures in hooded robes and illuminated only by burning black candles.

My first meeting was nothing of the sort.

Where I expected sour pusses, I found smiling faces.

Where I expected hooded figures and burning black candles I found only laughter and light.

And I found relief from a fatal malady. An obsession of the mind and an allergy of the body that I thought would never rub off on me from my father.

Never in a million years.

A member took me aside that night and said: "Misery is optional."

MISERY IS OPTIONAL.

Meaning I don't have to be miserable for one minute of my life.

I have a choice today.

And I still have that sage from 33 years ago as my dear friend. We choose not to be miserable, one day at a time.

Natalie certainly was not miserable when I began taking those baby steps toward recovery.

She was supportive, and most importantly, she was going to stay the course with me, even going so far as to go to *open meetings* with me.

But how, you wonder, did my father take this?

What did he say about my new way of walkin' and my new way of talkin'?

A lot, actually, and I will tell you all about it in the next chapter, which I am dedicating to the man who guided me to *THOSE MEETINGS* in the first place: my uncle, Vince Smith.

Chapter Twenty-Three: Uncle Vince

Exactly 10 years before I darkened the door of one of *THOSE MEETINGS*, I found myself in Uncle Vince's living room in Florida drinking beer with two of his three sons.

Now, I knew from Dad that Uncle Vince had been one of his most formidable drinking buddies in the day.

Vince Smith was a man who could hold his liquor while cranking out sports stories for the newspapers in Philadelphia.

Uncle Vince was exactly what I wanted to become: a two-fisted reporter.

Oh yes!

So I asked Uncle Vince to join us.

Have a beer.

Come on.

Hey, we were having a good time, so why shouldn't he?

And he was the one who loomed larger-than-life in family lore as a real drinker.

But there he was sitting in the corner of his Florida living room sipping coffee.

COFFEE!!!!

Not my idea of a party drink.

Not then, and not even now.

So I repeated my invitation: "Want a beer, Uncle Vince?"

"No thanks," he said.

He smiled.

I didn't.

"Come on, Uncle Vince, have a beer."

I did not feel comfortable drinking when anyone else in the room was not drinking.

So I gave my uncle my most winning look.

"Come on."

"No, thanks."

I saw that my cousins were trying to wave me off, but I would not be dissuaded.

I wanted my party-guy of an uncle to have a beer with me.

Gol-darn it!

Nope.

Uncle Vince was happy with his coffee.

So I was a complete pain in the ass and persisted with my insistence.

Finally Uncle Vince put down his coffee, looked me straight in the eye, and said: "I'm off the sauce."

Or words to that effect.

The effect on me was that of an electric eel crawling up my spine.

"Off the sauce. You mean—"

"I'm alcoholic. I go to—"

Yep: *THOSE MEETIINGS.*

Can't seem to stay away from those meetings.

I dropped the rock right then and there and said no more about Uncle Vince having a beer with us, and I tried mightily to make my beer taste anything but bitter.

Another mustard seed had been planted.

And from that humble seed a mighty bush of sobriety would spring some 11 years later, leading me to attend *THOSE MEETINGS* in venues like the *Mustard Seed* in Chicago.

Uncle Vince altered my drinking that day in Florida in 1971.

I felt his experience, strength, and hope every time I lifted a drink to my lips after that night.

He haunted me with his smile and his coffee and his ability to sit placidly while others about him were drinking.

Hmmmmm!!!!

So when I got sober, I wrote to Uncle Vince and told him what I had done, and he wrote back and said I should abide by some simple rules:

Don't drink,

Go to meetings,

Get a sponsor,

Work the steps.

The usual good, orderly directions.

And all from a member of the family.

Which brings us back to the head of my family, Dear Old Dad:

I was a zealot when I first got sober.

No denying.

And I had a sponsor who cut me to the quick by noting that my family was afflicted with the disease and that it would claim my father before his 70th birthday.

My sponsor, *Ohio Joe*, ordered me to make a stink.

State my case for recovery.

And I did.

And the result was none too pretty.

The word *pariah* come to mind?

Oh yeah, I was cast out after my righteous declarations on behalf of sobriety, and so Natalie and I celebrated Easter and Thanksgiving in 1982 with sober friends.

With my new family of like-minded people.

I was told to take my moral crusade elsewhere, and I did.

But then along came Christmas, Dad's favorite holiday by far.

He couldn't stand the thought of the family being apart at Christmas, so he reached out, indirectly, but he reached out nonetheless, and so Natalie and I went to 1645 W. 106th Street for Christmas.

My sobriety and Dad's drinking were the twin elephants in the living room.

Nothing was said about either subject, but Dad did offer me all the Canada Dry Ginger Ale I wanted.

And then some.

And so it went, and the uneasy truce continued until Mom and Dad took a trip down to Florida to visit Uncle Vince and Aunt Carol. By way of explanation, Vince Smith married Dad's middle sister, Carol, hence the connection.

Anyway, Dad had a long talk with his old pal and brother-in-law, Vince Smith, about me and my new way of walkin' and new way of talkin'.

Uncle Vince explained in a letter that he laid it all out to his lifelong friend Jimmy McKelvy.

Dad was on board.

Not that Dad was suddenly going to go to *THOSE MEETINGS*.

Nothing of that sort.

But Dad understood where I was and where I was going, and he let Uncle Vince know that he wanted me to feel welcome at family gatherings.

And so I was.

Why, I remember a great day at Wrigley Field in 1983 with Dad and my brother and a friend from the neighborhood and a friend from *THOSE MEETINGS*.

We enjoyed a great afternoon of day baseball (is there anything better on the planet than day baseball?), and those who were so inclined kept the beer man coming back for more sales.

Yeah, I wished my Dad would join me for a meeting or two and maybe discover some of the honesty, openness, and willingness that I was finding at *THOSE MEETINGS*.

But I didn't badger him or give my salesman of a father the hard sell.

I just showed him that I could enjoy a Cubs game without a drink.

Why I even wore a white straw hat that prompted the beer man to declare: "Nice sky piece."

Nice sky piece, indeed.

I was stylin', and I was at peace with the new family order.

But I was also mindful of *Ohio Joe's* prediction that my father would not live to see 70.

"The disease," *Ohio Joe* said before he died, "is going to kill your father in his 60s. Mark my word."

Sadly, we will mark *Ohio Joe's* word in the next, and final, chapter.

Chapter Twenty-Four: Comin' Home

"It's tough to lose your Daddy."

Those were Cousin Dave's words to my brother and me after we bore our father's body out of the Church of the Mediator on September 17, 1985.

Dad, as *Ohio Joe* had predicted, had died well before 70, at 67 on September 13, 1985.

It was the booze all right.

But who am I to say?

What I will say is that I saw signs of my father's demise on Thanksgiving Day, 1983.

I had not seen Dad for a good long while. Probably not since that Cubs game earlier that year.

Yeah, we had our uneasy truce, but my new-found sobriety had let air out of our tires.

It stood in our way.

Plain and simple.

No more drinking the trifecta.

No more getting looped together in the Loop.

We were not to stagger from Binyon's to the Berghoff to Miller's Pub again.

So, I was the unseen son.

The prodigal who had gone off and chosen *THOSE MEETINGS* over stingers and Bloody Marys and other bottled birthrights.

But then came the call to gather for Thanksgiving around the dining room table at 1645 W. 106th Street, and we answered.

And when we walked into *Mac's Bar & Grill* that Thanksgiving Day, I was shocked by my father's emaciated appearance.

He looked like the skeletal remains of those unfortunate souls who had survived imprisonment by the Japanese during World War II.

My Dad had always been a *big* guy.

He had been a man of *substance*.

Overweight?

Yes.

Hefty?

Oh yeah.

Husky?

Definitely.

Dad was never fat exactly, but he was, for the longest time, full of face and just *solid*.

And there he was on Thanksgiving looking like he had been locked in a sauna for a month.

I was shocked and didn't know what to say.

But both Mom and Dad expected me to say something, so I said: "Dad, you've lost weight."

Dad smiled, put his electrolarynx— his voice box—to his neck and said: "I was wondering if you'd notice."

Mom just stood there, looking nervous.

Ditto my brother and sister.

There was talk of Dad just having been sick at a recent Penn State/Notre Dame football game at Notre Dame, and, yes, there was **THE BIG C** staring at us again.

This time it was cancer of the esophagus.

Not good.

No siree, Bob.

Dad got the definitive diagnosis not long after that Thanksgiving dinner, and Natalie and I went to see him at the good, big hospital near the Loop where he was being held.

Excuse me, where he was being treated.

We treat people for cancer, don't we?

Sure we do.

We slash and burn and carve and cut and—we really haven't come very far from the days of bloodletting and leeching, have we?

Anyway, my Dad was scared.

Really frightened.

"I'm scared, Char," he said, after he hugged me.

My mouth moved, but no words emerged.

"You were in the seminary," Dad said. "You were trained for this kind of deal. Give me some words of comfort."

My mouth moved, but no words emerged.

I asked that Higher Power of mine for help, and all He said was: *You know what to say.*

So I said, "Let's take this a day at a time, Dad. Maybe, maybe, maybe—"

But there was no maybe.

Just a sure and certain march to the operating room at the good, big hospital to basically hollow Dad out.

When they were done carving on him, he was physically half of the Dad I had always known.

I am sorry to say I had to work in Evanston for a good, big corporation that supplied this, that, and everything to hospitals, so I was not there with Mom and my brother and sister at the hospital, waiting to see Dad on the other side of that hours-long operation to save him from the cancer that was galloping through his guts.

Well, Dear Old Dad survived the surgery, and he did live each and every day left to him with all the gusto he could muster.

I give my father infinite credit for his resilience in the face of sure and certain doom.

He fought back, and he went to the ballpark and came up to Evanston to have lunch with me while I was working for that now-defunct hospital supplier.

Dad was really proud of me when I had that job—in corporate public affairs, and he would have loved to see my office, but the company had a closed office policy, meaning that family and friends were not welcome to drop up for a tour.

The closest Dad got to my corporate life was the lobby of that building in downtown Evanston where there was a display of all the products the company supplied to hospitals.

That was good enough for Dad.

He saw that his oldest was finally making something of himself, and he approved.

But before he departed this mortal coil, I departed the good, big hospital supplier to make my way as a freelance writer.

I did well, and, ironically, I succeeded because I had as a major client a leading division of the good, big hospital supplier.

Oh, and a cookie company.

That's right: I was *Mister Cookie.*

And I got that cookie company some great publicity, and I was trying to get them even more when Dad took to his bed on the second floor at 1645 W. 106th Street and began his final approach to that naval air station in the sky.

Dad's surviving two sisters—Aunt Carol and Aunt Cynie—had come to see him and say good-bye.

I know the three of them were haunted by the death in 1954 of their sister Sally from leukemia. I was, too, even though I only knew my Aunt Sally for a few short years. (Still, I have a picture over my desk of her holding me, in Ship Bottom, New Jersey.)

Aunt Sally was Mom's best friend, and she was the second of the four *McKelvy Children* born to Carolyn Scovel and Eugene Adams McKelvy. In order of appearance: Jimmy, Sally, Carol, and Cynie.

They were famous for saying: *We ARE the McKelvy Children.*

Thanks to Aunt Cynie, my brother, sister, and I have since become famous for making the same bold declaration.

But I digress, when I should be moving forward.

Forward to my father's death on Friday the 13th, in September of 1985.

Hoooo, it's hard to write about, even now.

But write about it I must, because: *Your Dad's your Dad.* Right?

So, let's say I lied to you when I said this was the last chapter. This isn't the last chapter.

Not by a long shot.

I need to take a walk and have a talk with my Higher Power.

Then I'll be back with more.

Okay?

Thanks.

Chapter Twenty-Five: *"Oh! My Pa-Pa"*

Which would you rather have: the English lyrics or the German?

English, you say?

Sehr gut!

And here, in English, is the song that reduced my father to tears every time he heard it, especially when sung by Eddie Fisher with Hugo Winterhalter's orchestra and chorus:

Oh, my Papa, to me he was so wonderful,
Oh, my Papa, to me he was so good.
No one could be so gentle and so lovable,
Oh, my Papa, he always understood.
Oh, my Papa, so funny, so adorable,
Always the clown so funny in his way.
Oh, my Papa, to me he was so wonderful.
Deep in my heart I miss him so today.

Correct me if I'm wrong, but I believe we were returning from a family vacation to Clam Lake, Wisconsin when I first heard that song on the radio. Or maybe I had heard it before, but I will forever associate Dad and the German song John Turner and Geoffrey Parsons adapted into English with Wisconsin, that most German of American States.

We were cruising along in our big American hunk of steel when Eddie Fisher crooned about his papa being so wonderful.

Dad disappeared.

I don't mean he vanished from sight, but he was transfixed at the steering wheel as Eddie Fisher sang his number-one hit from 1954.

I remember sitting in the passenger seat and staring at my lachrymose father.

What in the world?

Was Eddie Fisher making my father think of his father, who had died of a heart attack at the age of 68 in 1948?

I had never talked to Dad about his Dad, Eugene Adams McKelvy, aka: EA.

My grandfather EA was as much a mystery to me as the Periodic Table of the Elements had been in Mrs. McKenzie's chemistry class at Morgan Park High School.

Meaning that I had no idea what kind of relationship my father had with his father.

What in the world?

Indeed:

What in the world?

Dad didn't explain his tears over a sentimental ditty that had begun as a German song as related by a young woman remembering her beloved, once-famous clown father.

Go figure.

And go figure how a *dirty-little-Jap-hating* U.S. naval officer like my father would go to pieces every time he listened to Giacomo Puccini's *Madama Butterfly*.

Madam Butterfly, right?

Yes, that would be the tragic opera about a geisha who gives up everything for the U.S. naval officer who promises her the world. When Lieutenant Pinkerton reneges on his promise, Madam Butterfly commits suicide with her father's knife.

Puccini does not portray the U.S. Navy and Americans in a positive light in his three-act opera. Why, we had an opera-loving friend, Julie Holmes, who absolutely refused to watch *Madam Butterfly* with us because it was so anti-American, and because she had proudly served overseas with the U.S. Department of State. Julie had *Butterfly* in her amazing collection of operas, but Julie wouldn't even glance at the screen when we watched it in her living room, even though it featured her beloved Plácido Domingo as Lt. Pinkerton.

Julie left us in 2009, and I wonder if she and Dad have met in the *Great Bye-and-Bye,* and if they have perchance discussed Puccini's masterpiece.

I would love to be a fly on that heavenly wall and eavesdrop on that conversation.

I would be particularly interested in hearing Dad say why he loved *Madam Butterfly* so much.

Why he kept an LP of the opera's highlights in our stereo cabinet and why he loved to play it when he was in his cups?

And when wasn't he in his cups?

Why *Madam Butterfly?*

Why *Oh! My Pa-Pa?*

Dad never said.

Well, he did.

He turned on the water works when he heard either work, especially Butterfly's death aria, *Con onor muore.*

Dad was absolutely unapproachable when he listened to that music.

I learned not to approach him at such times.

But I watched.

And I wondered.

Hmmm.

Where is he, and why these two works?

Hmmm.

I wish I could tell you.

I know that my father experienced great tragedy in his life:

-He lost his father in 1948, and—

-He lost the love of his young life on November 28, 1942 when she and 491 others perished in the deadliest nightclub fire in history, at the Coconut Grove in Boston.

Dad had been detained by Navy duties, and so when he arrived to meet his lady for their date at Boston's premiere nightclub, the Coconut Grove was engulfed in flames and panicked patrons were trampling one another to death in a mad scramble to flee the main entrance, a single revolving door rendered useless in the mayhem.

I'm sure Dad talked about Coconut Grove.

But not to me.

I would have liked to have heard what it was like for him that night to arrive in uniform looking forward to a lovely evening with his sweetheart with the other Thanksgiving weekend revelers and the football fans who had just seen Holy Cross upset Boston College 55-12.

Dad never spoke of any of this—at least not to me.

I had to look up the Coconut Grove Fire on *Wikipedia, the free encyclopedia.*

But *Wikipedia* didn't provide the name of Dad's sweetheart.

Just the fact that official reports stated "that the fire started at about 10:15 p.m. in the dark Melody Lounge downstairs."

Want to hear the rest of it?

I sure do.

Here it is, straight from *Wikipedia:*

A young pianist and singer, Goody Goodelle, was performing on a revolving stage, surrounded by artificial palm trees. It was believed that a young man, possibly a soldier, had removed a light bulb in order to give himself privacy while kissing his date. Stanley Tomaszewski—a 16-year-old busboy—was instructed to put the light back on by retightening the bulb. As he attempted to tighten the light bulb in its socket, the bulb fell from his hand. In the dimly-lit lounge, Tomaszewski, unable to see the socket, lit a match to illuminate the area, found the socket, extinguished the match, and replaced the bulb. Almost immediately, patrons saw something ignite in the canopy of artificial palm fronds draped above the tables (although the official report doubts the connection between the match and the subsequent fire).

Despite waiters' efforts to douse the fire with water, it quickly spread along the fronds of the palm tree, igniting decorations on the walls and ceiling. Flames raced up the stairway to the main level, burning the hair of patrons stumbling up the stairs. A fireball burst across the central dance floor as the orchestra was beginning its evening show. Flames raced through the adjacent Caricature Bar, then down a corridor to the Broadway Lounge. Within five minutes, flames had spread to the main clubroom and the entire nightclub was ablaze.

As is common in panic situations, many patrons attempted to exit through the main entrance, the same way they had entered. The building's main entrance was a single revolving door, rendered useless as the panicked crowd scrambled for safety. Bodies piled up behind both sides of the revolving door, jamming it to the extent that firefighters had to dismantle it to enter. Later, after fire laws had tightened, it would become illegal to have only one revolving door as

*a main entrance without being flanked by outward opening doors
with panic bar openers attached, or have the revolving doors set up
so that the doors could fold against themselves in emergency
situations.*

*Other avenues of escape were similarly useless: side doors had
been bolted shut to prevent people from leaving without paying. A
plate glass window, which could have been smashed for escape, was
boarded up and unusable as an emergency exit. Other unlocked
doors, like the ones in the Broadway Lounge, opened inwards,
rendering them useless against the crush of people trying to escape.
Fire officials later testified that, had the doors swung outwards, at
least 300 lives could have been spared. Many young soldiers
perished in the disaster, as well as a newly married couple.*

*As night deepened, the temperature dropped. Water on
cobblestones froze. Hoses froze to the ground. Newspaper trucks
were appropriated as ambulances. From nearby bars, soldiers and
sailors raced to assist. On the street, firefighters lugged out bodies
and were treated for burned hands. Smoldering bodies, living and
dead, were hosed in icy water. Some victims had ingested fumes so
hot that when they inhaled cold air, as one firefighter put it, they
dropped like stones.*

*Later, during the cleanup of the building, firefighters found
several dead guests sitting in their seats, with drinks in their hands.
They had been overcome so quickly by fire and toxic smoke that they
hadn't had time to move.*

Dad never said a word of any of this to me.

To others, yes, and from them I know that he was one of
those who helped lug out smoldering bodies, living and dead.

I know from Dad's confidantes that he also had to go and
identify his sweetheart at a makeshift morgue after the fire.

But that's it.

I don't even know her name.

Dad never said.

Oh! My Pa-Pa.

Chapter Twenty-Six: A Lasting Goodbye

Aunt Carol and Aunt Cynie said goodbye to their big brother, and then they flew back to their respective homes in Florida and Pennsylvania.

Dad was still at the good, big hospital, and he was using his electrolarynx to good effect by participating in a support group of fellow cancer patients.

My Dad, the group-therapy guy.

Who knew?

Well, God did.

He had heard my prayer back in 1964 when I was in the boy scouts. I had begged God to get Dad to *THOSE MEETINGS,* and God had not said no to my request.

He had merely said: "Not now."

Meaning, much, much, much later—

In 1985.

Attendance at the cancer-support group was limited to the patients and their significant others.

So Mom went with Dad, and she told me I should be so very proud of him because he was such a comfort to the other patients, including one who was—ready for this—both Jewish and gay.

Wow!

Who knew?

I often picture my movie-star-handsome father sitting in his hospital robe in that circle of cancer patients.

He reflects on something someone has said.

He gets that thoughtful look on his face.

He lifts his voice box from Aurex to his neck.

He says—

Sorry, I don't know what he says.

What he said.

But I was there that September afternoon at 1645 W. 106th Street after riding down from the North Side on a Chicago Transit Authority train to a terminal east of Beverly.

I had to hop a bus to get home, but that was all right because all that waiting and riding gave me time to think about whom I was about to see and what I was about to say to him.

My Dad.

The man in the bed upstairs in the master bedroom.

James Scovel McKelvy, born June 15, 1918, and waiting to die on September 13, 1985.

My Dad.

Calm as a cucumber.

My Dad.

O Mein Papa.

Excuse me:

Oh! My Pa-Pa.

Mom and Pudah—yes, Pudah was there to the end—said Dad was waiting to see me, and so I walked up past the first landing and then the second and down the hall and went into the room he shared with Mom, and there he was in his bed, just—I don't know—chillin'?

Yeah, pretty much.

Just days away from death's door, and my Pa-Pa was chillin'.

I thought:

Dad, I know you've been meaning to teach me how to live, and now you're teaching me how to die.

With quiet dignity.

With peace.

So we talked.

I know we watched the Chicago Bears and discussed their prospects for the post season.

(And, wouldn't you know it, the Monsters of the Midway went and demolished the New England Patriots 46-10 in Super Bowl XX on January 26, 1986 at the Louisiana Superdome in New Orleans. I know Dad was cheering with all the saints in heaven, and I so much felt his presence days later in downtown Chicago when the city paraded da' Bears along LaSalle Street where Dad had worked for General Refractories.)

So, yeah, we talked Bears.

And football.

And of this, and of that.

And when it was time for me to go back to the North Side with Natalie, I bent over the bed, kissed Dad on the forehead, and said: "I love you, Dad."

He blinked back his tears, and I left.

And he died not so very long thereafter.

And before lapsing into the coma that would take him out, Dad fussed mightily with my poor sister over his voice box.

He wanted to be sure his voice box was working properly.

That the batteries were charged.

He fussed and fussed and fussed.

His last words were with freighted worry over his artificial voice.

The voice that had informed his very presence since 1957.

When I said my final goodbye to Dad the night he died, he was no longer talking by any means.

His eyes were closed and his breathing was heading for the shallows.

I thought of staying the night with him.

Keeping watch.

But Natalie said we needed to get home in the family car. We didn't have a car of our own then, and—

Well, we went back to the North Side to await THE CALL.

Mom awakened us with it at—I don't know—seven or so the morning of the 13th.

"Your father's gone," she said.

I cried.

That's all I remember saying.

And I am sure I told Mom we would be "down" in a few hours.

But first I had to pay a special tribute to the man who had taught me to respect the Atlantic Ocean and Lake Michigan.

I went for a swim with Natalie at the Lincoln-Belmont YMCA.

And then I went with Natalie to sit shiva for my father.

For the man I had known as my father from May 7, 1950 to September 13, 1985.

Oh! My Pa-Pa.

Chapter Twenty-Seven: Catholic Content

All right, already:

I did promise I would say much more about my journey from Canterbury to Rome, so let me say it now.

And I can say it all best if I quote directly from an article I wrote for the December 2006 edition of *The Catholic Yearbook.*

To wit:

When people ask me when I decided to become a Catholic, I tell them it was on a breathtaking Friday evening in August 1967. Granted I was not received into the faith until December 1998, but I truly embarked on the road to conversion in 1967 at the age of 17 as I rode the train they called *The Empire Builder* to the Boy Scout World Jamboree in Farragut State Park, Idaho.

We entered the Rockies on the Sunday morning of our journey, so my roommate and I secured the best pair of seats in the dome car so we could take it all in. Then, an assistant scoutmaster appeared and announced that he was going to conduct a Protestant worship service in the dome car. My roommate and I were both cradle Episcopalians, but we said we could gladly stay and participate.

We were glad we did because it was a lovely little prayer service with scripture, psalms, and an attempt or two at singing. All while passing through some of the most splendid scenery in North America.

Then, after the Protestants had had their fill of that mobile chapel, another assistant scoutmaster, Father John Rice, SJ, appeared and said he was going to celebrate Sunday Mass for the Catholics in the troop. We asked if there was going to be an Anglican rite for us, and he said no, just the Protestant service and Catholic Mass.

"Well," I told him, "since we're members of the so-called *bridge church*, we should stay for Mass."

Father John welcomed us to stay and hoped that we would participate fully except for receiving the Eucharist.

That was fine with the two of us, since neither of us had ever been to a Catholic Mass. So, we stayed in our seats to witness a rite that was remarkably similar to the Holy

Communion Service we had grown up with in the Episcopal Church.

In the true spirit of Vatican II, Father John celebrated Mass in English while facing all of us. I remember that he welcomed one and all to the Lord's banquet and gave thanks for the splendor of God's creation that was unfolding around us.

When the Mass was ended, we remained at peace with the passing scenery, and I had Father John in a good place in my mind the following Friday afternoon when he came to my patrol's campsite at the Jamboree and said: "How would you like to go with me to Shabbat at the Israeli troop's campsite?"

I thought that Father John was taking ecumenism to a new level, but I was more than happy to go along because the so-called *Six Days' War* in June that year had flavored our World Jamboree in August. For one thing, Egypt, Jordan, and Syria, along with all the other Arab nations, had decided to boycott the Jamboree because of America's support of Israel in the war that had led to their humiliating defeat.

Having just fought a costly war of national survival, the Israelis were not inclined to send a large contingent of boy scouts to Idaho. So they sent one small troop of young men who were not only boy scouts but veterans of the *Six Days' War—Lions of Judah.*

I told Father John that I would be delighted to accompany him to witness what had to be a moving Shabbat. He assured me I would not regret it, and that it would be an experience I would hold in my heart for the rest of my days.

How right he was.

For what we encountered at the Israeli campsite on a luminous Friday evening in the breathtaking beauty of the Idaho panhandle was a truly biblical event.

Yes, there were those young Israeli scouts—*the Lions of Judah*—who were in their late teens like me, but who had *thousand-yard stares* that came from the heavy fighting needed to save their homeland from annihilation.

Then there was the local Jewish community that came in buses from as far as Spokane, Washington.

Father John encouraged me to drink it all in, and I certainly did as a woman alighted from one of the buses and burst into tears at the sight of the blue-and-white flag of a free and independent Israel snapping smartly in the Idaho breeze. She had a number tattooed on her forearm, and Father John did not need to explain its meaning to me (and, I hope and pray, I do not have to explain its meaning to you, dear reader).

After the shofar had been blown and the cantor had intoned the ancient prayer in Hebrew, Father John said I had seen the hand of God at work in the modern world.

I never forgot that awesome evening in August 1967, and I never will.

Eventually, I drifted away from the Episcopal Church and stopped going to church altogether.

Then a funny thing happened:

I found myself running past churches on Sunday mornings, longing for the spiritual sustenance offered inside.

It was the crystalline memory of witnessing biblical history with Father John Rice, SJ, that propelled me forward into full acceptance into the Catholic Church in 1998—13 years after my father's death and 15 years before my mother's departure.

I think Dad knew I would become a *mackerel-snapper* one day.

He knew I pal'd around with Casey and Bowline and all those other Catholic kids in the neighborhood.

Hey, his best friend in the whole world was a Catholic cop called Big John.

And, truth be told, I just know that I wouldn't have to shake the McKelvy family tree too hard to get a few Catholic apples to fall out of the upper branches.

And Mom?

Mom was there at Saint Agnes Church in Sawyer, Michigan when I was received into the Catholic Church in December 1998.

She didn't much like it, but she was there.

So that's my conversion story, and I'm stickin' with it.

And so allow me to offer a much belated but deeply heartfelt thank-you to the priest who put me on the right path, Father John, wherever you are!

It took me a while, but I finally found my way home, thanks to you.

Afterword

Two things, Dad.

Two little things for you to read, apropos your admonition to me that afternoon so long ago at the Beverly House on Vincennes.

Remember?

I do, because you took me aside after one of our long, liquid luncheons and told me: "You kids take care of your mother after I'm gone. After all she's done for you, you take care of her. You understand?"

Oh, I understood all right.

Only too well.

So, I'd like to share these two little things with you, Dad.

First, a piece I wrote for *The Beverly Review* that appeared in that august neighborhood weekly on November 27, 1996, and—

Second, the eulogy I delivered in Illinois, Michigan, **AND** Pennsylvania for your wife of 36 years.

I believe we honored your wishes, Dad.

I believe we right honorably honored both you and your wife, our mother, Hannah Dick Macfarlan McKelvy.

So settle back on your cloud, Dad, and attend to the following:

1. Page 10, *The Beverly Review November 27, 1996*
Beverly memories prove there's no place like home
by Charles McKelvy

She's leaving home after all these years.

She being my mother, and home being the two-story brick house on 106th Street in Beverly where I celebrated my sixth birthday in 1956 just after the family moved from a cramped apartment in South Shore.

Mom is moving in November to a single-story bungalow on 101st Street. It's up the hill from Longwood Drive and right next door to my sister, Missy, and her family.

Mom is a 70-something widow with a bad hip and wants to be secure in her lodgings. The move makes perfect sense, and everyone agrees that it's for the best.

But there remains, or remained, the business of saying goodbye to the old house on 106th Street.

As I said, we moved there in 1956 when I was 6 and my brother was 3. Missy was born the following year, in 1957, and my brother Don and I sold cupcakes and charged admission to see her when Mom brought her home from the hospital. (Mom still reminds us that we charged more for the cupcakes than admission to see Missy, but then new babies were commonplace on 106th Street in those days.)

When we moved in there were two blue spruces in the backyard that were barely taller than my brother and me. Now the first branches are beyond my reach. Yes, the oaks are all still there, towering over the yard and shedding their acorns and leaves.

Time was when we would rake the leaves into the gutter and flagrantly burn them. (Where I live now in Michigan people still burn leaves the old-fashioned way, and it really takes me back to the old home.) Then, when 106th Street was enveloped in smoke, we'd ride back and forth on our bikes, pretending we were World War II fighter pilots high over Germany.

In winter, we'd craft our version of a bobsled run out of huge snowballs and ample doses of water from a bucket. The run took advantage of the small hill in front of the old family house and descended right into 106th Street. When all was ready, we'd test our handiwork by mounting little Missy in a "flying saucer" and rocketing her downhill.

Mom would watch in horror from the other side of the big picture window that framed our living room, but Missy always made it safely to the other side of 106th Street. And we'd always post somebody to watch for cars. Or almost always.

There didn't seem to be much traffic in those days, and people tended to drive slower than they do now. I guess there was less agitated monotony back in the '60s.

Anyway, we all did a lot of great living in that old house on 106th Street. I returned recently to help Mom pack and spend a final night in my old bedroom.

The only things missing were my brother Don (who still snores, I bet); our late, great dog Cindy; the noisy night shift at the now abandoned Chicago Bridge & Iron plant on Vincennes Avenue; and explosive arguments between the Lithuanian cop (that would be *Big John*, of course) and his Irish wife who lived next door.

All was quiet and peaceful on my last night in the old house. But I lay awake half the night just the same remembering and savoring and saying goodbye to the house where I grew up and:

-became a writer, and curled up with book after book borrowed from my parents' burgeoning shelves and the Walker Branch of the Chicago Public Library, and

-broke both wrists while trying to get a basketball down from the overhead garage door, and

-ran my Lionel train around the ping-pong table every winter, and

-left for the Navy, and came back from boy scout camp, and

-fought and made up with my brother and sister, and

-burned trash in the backyard before it was illegal, and

-had my first taste of liquor by borrowing a "wee dram" from Dad's scotch bottle and then replacing it with water. (He discovered the theft, of course, and said if I was going to drink his scotch, I should at least have the decency not to water it down when I was finished.)

Speaking of Dad, the house was truly his, and it was where he chose to die in 1985. I last spoke to him in that house, and I am happy to say they were words of love.

We call houses homes because we love them so.

And I loved every square inch of that great old house on 106th Street.

It seemed so big to me in the spring of 1956 when we first moved there from that little apartment in South Shore.

And it seemed so big to me still in the fall of 1996 when I came home to say goodbye.

So big because it was my home for nearly 20 years, and so big because it will always be home in my heart.

2. Then, this, the eulogy I delivered for Mom in Chicago, Illinois; Bridgman, Michigan, and Pittsburgh, Pennsylvania:

Hannah Dick Macfarlan McKelvy
May 29, 1921-June 4, 2014

Picture this:

We are settled in the second row, stage right, at Orchestra Hall, and the Chicago Symphony Orchestra—arguably one of the best in the world—is tuned and ready to deliver yet another amazing performance under the baton of their Italian stallion of a music director, Riccardo Muti.

Devices have been silenced, and the full house awaits in silent anticipation for Maestro Muti to enter stage right, right over our heads.

And then, when a dropping pin would bust the mood, the shy lady in seat B7, the one and only Hannah Dick Macfarlan McKelvy, says in that full voice of hers—loud enough for the cabbies on Michigan Avenue to hear:

Where's the big guy?!?

The pin dropped, and then the big guy himself appeared, and, being the good Italian son that he is, he smiled down on Momma McKelvy as he strode to the podium.

Mom nodded approvingly and allowed as how the big guy could get on with the show, and he did.

And Maestro Muti did, indeed, smile down at Mom when it was all over, and, despite her 90-something years, she hauled herself to her feet to join the standing ovation.

Speaking of which, don't you all think it's time we gave Hannah Dick Macfarlan McKelvy a standing ovation for her outstanding 93-year run?

(Pause for standing ovation.)

If anyone deserves a standing ovation, it is the second child of Kenneth and Mary Louise Macfarlan, wife of James Scovel McKelvy, mother of Chucky, Ducky, and Missy; colorful mother-in-law of Natalie, Sam, and Stu; grandmother of Jake, Sara, Annie, Nate, Meg, and Jim, and friend/confessor/mentor to all, especially here at Woodland Terrace.

By the way, Mom's love affair with classical music began as a child when her Aunt Teeney would take her, her sister

Molly, and cousin Doty, to children's concerts at the Philadelphia Philharmonic Orchestra. She studied the piano as a girl, and she took ballet lessons from a real Russian ballerina.

As the granddaughter of a Scottish immigrant, she loved the skirl of the pipes, and we surprised her on her 92nd birthday at Tabor Hill by having our piper, Leonard Sailor, blow out the pipes for her. Mom, of course, couldn't get enough of Leonard and his pipes, and do you know what she told him when he sat down to join us for dinner?

The next time I hear you play will be at my funeral.

But before she died, Leonard did come back and play for Mom here at Woodland Terrace, and she insisted on going to the Blossomtime Parade in Saint Joe in 2013 and 2014 just to hear Leonard and his pipe-and-drum band. And, Leonard, she's making it abundantly clear to me that she was tickled pink by your piping Wednesday morning at the Church of the Holy Nativity in Chicago.

Mom was—and is—mad about music.

When we took her to a bluegrass festival in Niles along the Saint Joe River, she confessed that she wasn't familiar with the genre. But when they started a pickin' and a strummin' that old mountain music, Hannah Dick Macfarlan McKelvy was grinning from ear to ear and tapping her foot in perfect harmony.

And on June 6, when Sara, Natalie, and I attended the final concert of our Chicago Symphony Orchestra series, Mom's favorite musician, violinist Susan Synnestvedt, took me aside during the intermission and said Mom was her favorite patron—her *where's the big guy?* outbursts notwithstanding.

Mom celebrated her 93rd birthday just days before she went to join the ancestors, and she did it in style by taking the family on a culinary tour of Southwest Michigan even though she wasn't feeling so well.

But she rallied. "We're going to Tabor Hill," she said.

And we went to the Tabor Hill Winery and Restaurant to celebrate the birthday of one of life's true originals.

When Dickie—that's right, Dickie—was 9 years old, she took the Pennsylvania Railroad to Atlantic City with her Uncle Donald—Brother Donald is holding up Uncle Donald's ring in Florida as I speak—and her big sister, Molly.

As they were walking along the famous boardwalk, Uncle Donald saw that they were offering seaplane rides and told his two lovely nieces that he would gladly treat the braver of the two to a ride over the Atlantic Ocean.

Molly wanted none of that, but little Dickie slid right into that open cockpit and went for the ride of her life over the boardwalk, and piers, and open ocean.

As scared as she was, Mom loved it, and thus began her lifelong love of travel and adventure.

Duck and Miss, do you remember the Sunday drives Mom would take us on after church?

And when we acted up, she would say: "I don't know why I take you kids to church."

Mom, you took us to church so we would be in church Wednesday and at this prayerful gathering right now, celebrating your wonderful life and your non-stop travels.

Mom would just go, and we would just follow.

One fine September morn in the Year of Our Lord 2010, I asked Mom as I was driving her to a doctor's appointment in Tinley Park, Illinois: "Mom, would you like to move to Michigan?"

She replied without hesitation: "Sure."

And we surely moved Hannah Dick Macfarlan McKelvy right here to Woodland Terrace on October 30, 2010, and she lived happily here until Wednesday, June 4, 2014, when she died in her room at Dogwood surrounded by her loving family and beloved aides at 9:40 p.m.

To return the favor for all those wonderful Sunday drives when we were kids, I took to taking Mom, the newly minted Michigander, on drives all over Southwest Michigan. Mom was a quick study and soon was telling family members: "Those are the grapes, and those are blueberries, and those are apples, and that's corn, and that's soybeans."

Mom loved to watch the fall harvest, and she most especially delighted in the spring planting, signifying renewal of life.

Mom fittingly went to eternal life in the spring, planting herself forever in our hearts, and preparing a place for us in the beautiful vineyards of the *Sweet Bye-and-Bye*.

Mom is traveling the heavens over because she was such a traveler here:

Mom took Missy to Bermuda by ship, and she took Sara to Washington, D.C. by train, and she took to visiting Duck and Sam and Jake and Nate at each and every one of their postings. Mom insisted we take her on a farewell tour of her native Pennsylvania in 2011 so she could see her beloved Bobo and Annie and cousin Doty and sister-in-law Cynie, and she went to Disney World with Sara, Annie, Meg, and Jim, and one time, when we were returning from one of our countless trips back to Pennsylvania, Mom told me, a newly minted driver, to get off the turnpike and take the backroads across the Keystone State. "This is the real America," she said. "Plus, you should learn how to drive on a two-lane highway."

Mom, thanks to you, I still get off the interstate and drive the two-lane highways of America with the skill and alertness you taught me.

Nana sailed the Seven Seas, set foot on six of the seven continents, and she had a Neptune Party on the *QE2* when she crossed the equator on her cruise to New Zealand and Australia.

And, yes, at the age of 86 in 2007, Mother flew to Mother Russia and told Putin where to stick it.

She lived as long as she wanted to, and she wanted to as long as she lived.

And I know she is taking a heavenly cruise right now with a Dewer's on the rocks in hand and telling me:

Wind it up, Charley, me boy. No souls are saved after 20 minutes.

So I will wind it up, and I will speak on her behalf by inviting each and every one of you to continue sharing memories of Hannah Dick Macfarlan McKelvy every time she comes to mind.

And she'll come to mind every time you look at the heavens and see that angel with the Dewer's on the rocks sitting on cloud B7 and loudly demanding to know:

Where's the big guy?!?

So there you have it, Dad.

Two little things for you to read.

We good?

Good.

Charles McKelvy plays a Buffet Crampon RC Bb Clarinet.